A WYATT BOOK *for*

W

— ST. —
MARTIN'S
PRESS

THE ASSOCIATION OF THE BAR
OF THE CITY OF NEW YORK

and

Kevin Thomas Duffy, Marvin E. Frankel,
Stephen Gillers, Norman L. Greene,
Daniel J. Kornstein, and Jeanne A. Roberts

THE
ELSINORE
APPEAL

People v. Hamlet

A WYATT BOOK *for*
ST. MARTIN'S PRESS
New York

THE ELSINORE APPEAL: *People v. Hamlet*. Copyright © 1996 by
The Association of the Bar of the City of New York.

Production Editor: David Stanford Burr

Library of Congress Cataloging-in-Publication Data

The Elsinore appeal : People vs. Hamlet / the Association of the Bar
    of the City of New York ; Kevin Thomas Duffy . . . [et al.].
            p.   cm.
    "A Wyatt book for St. Martin's Press."
    Includes text of Hamlet.
    ISBN 0-312-14327-3
    1. Shakespeare, William, 1564–1616. Hamlet.
    2. Guilt (Law) in literature.   3. Shakespeare, William,
    1564–1616—Characters—Hamlet.   4. Mental illness
    in literature.   5. Shakespeare, William, 1564–1616—
    Characters—Mentally ill.   6. Shakespeare, William,
    1564–1616—Knowledge—Law. I. Duffy, Kevin Thomas.
    II. Association of the Bar of the City of New York.
    III. Shakespeare, William, 1564–1616. Hamlet.
    PR2807.E57   1996
    822.3'3—dc20   96-6491
                                                   CIP

First edition: October 1996

10   9   8   7   6   5   4   3   2   1

Book design by Jennifer Ann Daddio

CONTENTS

FOREWORD

The Elsinore Appeal is a result of the extraordinary efforts and imagination of the Committee on Lectures and Continuing Education (the "L.A.C.E." Committee) of the Association of the Bar of the City of New York. As Chair of the L.A.C.E. Committee, I watched The Elsinore Appeal develop from literally nothing but an idea to the spectacular program presented in this volume.

To understand truly how this program came into being, it is important to understand a bit about the Association and how its committees work. The Association, housed in a landmark building, has more than 20,000 members worldwide and over 180 committees. Through the efforts of its committees, the Association has a 125-year tradition of civic activism and public service while providing its members with the tools and opportunity for professional development.

The L.A.C.E. Committee supervises the programs presented by the Association's committees and, beyond that, produces programs of its own. Every year, the Association sponsors nearly 200 programs on legal and policy issues featuring scholars, government officials, representatives of business and other disciplines, members of the bench and bar, and the public. The range of programs the Association presents is truly remarkable. In the past year, our programs have ranged from detailed presentations of technical legal topics, to a forum on capital punishment featuring John Cardinal O'Connor, to The Elsinore Appeal.

These programs get their life from the committee members, all of whom are volunteers. The L.A.C.E. Committee, as well as the other committees that produce and publicize the programs, rely heavily on the creative efforts and time of the members and the Association staff. Each program begins with an idea and a decision to carry it out. Ideas are floated regularly, but only a few have legs sufficient to generate enough enthusiasm to command the energies of the membership. Such was the feeling generated during the development of The Elsinore Appeal. From the formatting of the program, to the selection of the speakers and development of the briefs and legal arguments, the enthusiasm built on itself, stimulated by the excellent subcommittee, chaired by Ellen B. Simon, that organized the program. I also want to thank the other members of her subcommittee, Eliot P. Green, Philip T. Temple, Stephen F. Selig, and L. Priscilla Hall, as well as Martha Harris, an Association staff lawyer who not only assisted with the program planning but was instrumental in arranging for the program to become this publication.

To delight, to educate, to motivate, to reform—these are all goals of Association programs, some more, some less. The Elsinore Appeal is one of our jewels, a truly unscripted slice of perfection— spontaneous, joyous, and fast-moving. Although we cannot bring you the laughter of hundreds of enthusiastic lawyers such as never before may have been heard in the Great Hall of the Association, we can bring you the lightning wit of the participants, who treated the fictional issues as if they were real.

—NORMAN L. GREENE

ROYAL DANISH COURT OF APPEALS
FOR THE ELSINORE CIRCUIT

STATE OF DENMARK,

APPELLEE,

against

HAMLET, PRINCE OF DENMARK,

APPELLANT

APPELLANT'S BRIEF

DANIEL J. KORNSTEIN
Attorney for Appellant

TABLE OF CONTENTS

Only rarely—once every four hundred years or so—does a criminal case come along so riddled with interesting error as this one. This is an appeal from six homicide convictions: five for second-degree murder (Laertes, Claudius, Polonius, and Rosencrantz, and Guildenstern), N.Y. Penal L. § 125.25, and one for second-degree manslaughter (Ophelia). N.Y. Penal L. § 125.15. On reexamining the judgment below, the Court, like one of the gravediggers who testified at trial, should ask, "But is this law?" (Hamlet, 5.1.21). The answer is "no," and each conviction should be reversed.

I.

SINCE HAMLET SUFFERED FROM DIMINISHED MENTAL CAPACITY, SUCH LACK OF CULPABILITY REQUIRES REVERSAL ON ALL COUNTS

At trial, appellant proved two defenses involving lack of culpability. First, he showed that at the time of the conduct alleged, as a result of mental disease or defect, he lacked substantial capacity to know or appreciate either (a) the nature and consequences of such conduct, or (b) that such conduct was wrong. See N.Y. Penal L. § 30.05. Second, defendant at the very least met the lesser standard of proving that he acted under the influence of extreme emotional disturbance for which there was a reasonable explanation or excuse from the defendant's point of view. N.Y. Penal L. § 125.25. Mental disease or defect is a complete defense to all charges, and emotional disturbance is a defense to second-degree murder and a mitigating factor for lesser offenses.

Appellant's mind was so disturbed and delusional that, as many witnesses observed, he talked irrationally, believed he saw and spoke to a ghost, and even explained that it was the ghost who told him to kill Claudius. Long referred to by the press as "the melancholy Dane," appellant, who testified at trial that he was at home recovering from a difficult and stressful year of studying law at Wittenberg University, was thrown further off balance and indeed was grief-stricken and severely depressed by his father's murder, his mother's quick marriage to the murderer—appellant's own uncle—and Ophelia's neglect of appellant's love. His emotional strain caused him to swing wildly between paralytic inaction and manic action. He even became suicidal.

The irrationality of such behavior hardly went unnoticed. Several of the decedents themselves had on a number of occasions called appellant "mad" and his actions "lunacy." Even Hamlet knew he was beset "with a sore distraction" (5.2.228). "What I have done," Hamlet says, referring to his killing of Polonius, "I here proclaim was madness. / Was't Hamlet wronged Laertes? Never Hamlet. / . . . His madness is poor Hamlet's enemy" (5.2.228–237).

In the trial court, the government tried to minimize this evidence by arguing that appellant's madness was feigned, that appellant himself at one point said he intended to put "an antic disposition on" (1.5.181). But for the government to stress that one, isolated utterance is not only to overlook appellant's entire psychological profile, but also to fail to distinguish between Hamlet's feigned madness and his real madness. When Hamlet chose, as in certain obvious encounters with Polonius, Claudius, Gertrude, and others, he brilliantly pretended to be irrational. At other times, also equally obvious, appellant's genuine grief, clinical depression and delusional thinking seriously impaired his mental capacity.

4

II.
Since Laertes died while attacking Hamlet with a poisoned sword in a duel initiated by Laertes, Hamlet acted in self-defense

Appellant meets all the requirements of self-defense in connection with the death of Laertes. Even Laertes conceded: "I am justly killed with mine own treachery" (5.2.310).

III.
Since Hamlet innocently and in good faith mistook Polonius, who hid himself in Hamlet's mother's bedroom, for someone else, possibly a malevolent intruder, burglar or murderer, Hamlet properly invoked the defense of justification

IV.
Since "heart balm" statutes have been abolished, and since Ophelia rejected Hamlet first, it would violate public policy to hold Hamlet criminally responsible for Ophelia's death

Presumably Ophelia committed suicide because she thought Hamlet no longer loved her. Perhaps he even broke a promise to marry her. However that may be, public policy bars fastening legal liability for her death upon Hamlet, either civilly or criminally.

Section 80-a of the New York Civil Rights Law abolishes any civil cause of action for breach of contract to marry. Although the criminal law recognizes that causing or aiding someone to commit suicide can be manslaughter (*N.Y. Penal L.* § 125.20) or murder (*N.Y. Penal L.* § 125.25), the conduct there contemplated is, to be sure, more than breaking a lover's heart, something more akin to Dr. Jack Kevorkian's much-publicized medically assisted suicides, or worse.

If male disappointment in romance is not a justification for homicide, *see, e.g. People v. Checo,* 194 A.D.2d 410, 599 N.Y.S.2d 244 (1st Dep't 1993); *People v. Hartsock,* 189 A.D.2d 991, 592 N.Y.S.2d 511 (3d Dep't 1993), neither should a female suicide resulting solely from such disappointment be a basis of criminal liability. Logic, symmetry, and feminism require no less.

Equally important is the sequence of events. Hamlet apparently lost interest in Ophelia only after Ophelia dumped him at Polonius's instructions. (1.3.91–137). Ophelia heeded her brother Laertes's warning and her father Polonius's command, and repelled Hamlet's romantic advances. (2.1.110–12). Polonius even went so far as to think that it was Ophelia's rejection of Hamlet that caused Hamlet's madness (2.1.112; 2.2.96–151; 3.1.179–81). In such circumstances, to blame Hamlet for Ophelia's suicide is irrational and against the weight of the evidence.

V.

SINCE ALL CONDUCT RELATING TO THE DEATHS OF ROSENCRANTZ AND GUILDENSTERN OCCURRED OUTSIDE DENMARK, THE TRIAL COURT HAD NO JURISDICTION TO TRY HAMLET FOR THEIR ALLEGED MURDERS

Acts charged must have been committed in this jurisdiction. *N.Y. Crim. Proc. L.* § 20.20. But the evidence shows that it was on a ship bound for England that Hamlet discovered that Rosencrantz and Guildenstern were escorting him there to be murdered. It was only then, aboard ship on the high seas, that Hamlet committed the acts complained of, *i.e.,* forging new documents from Claudius.

On this jurisdictional ground alone, his conviction for the deaths of Rosencrantz and Guildenstern should be reversed.

VI.

SINCE HAMLET, MORE VICTIM THAN WRONGDOER, ACTED PROPERLY IN BRINGING A MURDERER TO JUSTICE, AND FOUGHT TO RESIST REVENGE, THE INDICTMENT SHOULD BE DISMISSED "IN THE INTEREST OF JUSTICE"

This peculiar case is, in more senses than one, a tragedy that cries out for dismissal "in the interest of justice." *N.Y. Crim. Proc. L.* § 210.40. In addition to all the obvious mitigating factors surrounding Hamlet's lack of culpability, the history, character, and condition of appellant as himself a victim of a severely dysfunctional family and a disastrous first year at law school, other compelling considerations clearly demonstrate that appellant's conviction, a first offense, results in injustice.

Almost everyone assumes appellant had a duty to seek revenge, that he should have killed Claudius—a murderer, a regicide, and usurper of the throne—much sooner than he did. It is precisely appellant's delay in avenging his father's death that is often considered his basic weakness and that led to disaster. From this perspective, Hamlet did nothing wrong and everything right by killing Claudius. For doing so, for upholding the law, he should be praised not punished.

But this Court should also explore the thesis that Hamlet's delay does him credit as well, that appellant's indecision was an effort not to yield to the passion for revenge. Appellant's inner struggle then becomes an effort to transcend the lower morality of his time and environment and move beyond a rule of force and private vengeance to a modern rule of law. Appellant represents humanity's effort, faced with forces that would drag it backward, to ascend to a higher level. Hamlet reflects this civilizing function of law by struggling to resist the primitive call for revenge.

VII.

SINCE APPELLANT IS KING OF DENMARK, SOVEREIGN IMMUNITY REQUIRES REVERSAL ON ALL COUNTS

As the sole survivor of the royal family, Hamlet is the Danish monarch (1.2.108–09) and is therefore protected from criminal prosecutions by the doctrine of sovereign immunity. "The King can do no wrong."

When Goneril, daughter of King Lear, was asked if she admits having committed treason, her response was: "Say if I do, the laws are mine, not thine. / Who can arraign me for't?" *King Lear* (5.3.149–50). In an era of the divine right of kings, Hamlet, an absolute monarch, is "the deputy elected by the Lord." *Richard II* (3.2.53). "What subject can give sentence on his King?" *Id.* (4.1.108). At the least, the criminal case against King Hamlet should have been stayed as long as he is in office. *See* Def.'s Brief in *Jones v. Clinton.*

CONCLUSION

Appellant himself should have the final say on his own appeal. After four long centuries without an appeal, appellant was right to complain bitterly of "the law's delay." (3.1.73). After reviewing the prosecutor's sophistry, we respond, as appellant did to Polonius: "Words. Words. Words." (2.2.193). And, having exposed the "rotten" State's case, we ask of the State's counsel, as did appellant of another lawyer on another occasion: "Where be his quiddits now, his quillets, his cases, his tenures, and his tricks?" (5.1.99–100).

For the reasons given, the conviction below should be reversed.

Respectfully submitted,

Daniel J. Kornstein
Attorney for Appellant

ROYAL DANISH COURT OF APPEALS

FOR THE ELSINORE CIRCUIT

STATE OF DENMARK,

APPELLEE,

against

HAMLET, *FORMERLY* PRINCE OF DENMARK,

APPELLANT

APPELLEE'S BRIEF

STEPHEN GILLERS

Attorney for Appellee

OF COUNSEL: Hayley Baruk, Davida H. Isaacs, Christopher M. Locke, Linda A. Shashoua, Jonathan Wayne (admitted under the Elsinore Student Practice Rule)

TABLE OF CONTENTS

Hamlet, a serial killer, was unable to persuade the jury that madness or justification should excuse his bloody deeds. His own words betray his claim of madness. His justification defense fails on the facts. His immunity arguments are wrong on the law. His life sentence should be affirmed.

I.

THE JURY PROPERLY CONCLUDED THAT HAMLET DID NOT MEET HIS BURDEN OF PROVING INSANITY

Hamlet would have this Court recognize an entirely new defense to homicide: The Abused Prince Syndrome. It should not.

Penal Law § 40.15 gave Hamlet an "affirmative defense" if he suffered from a "mental disease or defect" that caused him to lack "substantial capacity to know or appreciate either [1] the nature and consequences of [his] conduct; or [2] that such conduct was wrong." The jury did not believe Hamlet or his paid experts.

Not only did Hamlet tell his friends that "I perchance hereafter shall think meet to put an antic disposition on" (1.5.180–81), he did so, and turned it on and off as it suited him.

When the king, queen, and others arrived for *The Murder of Gonzago,* Hamlet told Horatio, with whom he had been conversing in blank verse, "I must be idle. Get you a place." (3.2.89–90). Hamlet then "maneuvers a quick change into prose," as Harry Levin testified to the jury. (The Question of Hamlet, at 116.) Similar abrupt shifts occur when Hamlet encounters Ophelia (3.1.94) and when Osric approaches Hamlet and Horatio (5.2.82). These sudden changes from poetry to prose—accompanied by changes in the clarity of his language—prove that Hamlet did indeed "put an antic disposition on" as he predicted he would.

Following *The Murder of Gonzago,* when the queen exclaimed that Hamlet was suffering from "ecstasy" the defendant replied: "It is not madness / That I have uttered. Bring me to the test, And I the matter will reword which madness / Would gambol from." (3.4.148–51). Moments later, the defendant cautioned his mother against letting Claudius know "That I essentially am not in madness, But mad in craft." (3.4.194–95).

Hamlet's "madness" appeared only in the presence of persons he distrusted (the king, Rosencrantz and Guildenstern, Ophelia, Polonius). Even then, as others noted, "[t]hough this be madness, yet there is method in't" (Polonius) (2.2.205–06). Guildenstern recognized Hamlet's behavior as a "crafty madness" that "keeps [him] aloof." (3.1.8.). Hamlet was in fact quite reasonable in conversation with his schoolmates until he asked "Were you not sent for?" (2.2.275) and realized they were.

Hamlet's "antic disposition" protected him from Claudius while he tried to discover whether the "spirit that I have seen" is "the devil," who "hath power / T'assume a pleasing shape." (2.2.600-601). Harry Levin testified that Hamlet was "clearly thoughtsick rather than brainsick" (p. 113), and explained Hamlet's time-buying strategy as having successfully "forced" Claudius "against his habit, to continue more or less in Hamlet's medium." (p. 117.)

Like the jury, Claudius also doubted Hamlet's madness: "Nor what he spake, though it lack'd form a little, / Was not like madness. There's something in his soul / O'er which his melancholy sits on brood, / And I do not doubt the hatch and the disclose / Will be some danger." (3.1.166–70). Claudius used each of Polonius and Ophelia, and Rosencrantz and Guildenstern, to "pluck out the heart of [Hamlet's] mystery" (3.2.364–65), but to no avail.

Meanwhile, Hamlet crafted a brilliant and rational strategy to "catch the conscience of the King" (2.2.606) with evidence of his demeanor during *The Murder of Gonzago.* The jury could well have found that a man who could devise this plan and would not act on the Ghost's directive until he could ascertain its authenticity ("I'll have grounds / More relative than this") (2.2.604–605) knew that murder is wrong.

The jury rejected Hamlet's self-serving statement to Laertes. As the State argued, law student Hamlet was already planning his defense. He knew that his speech would be reported in *The Elsinore Bugle*, which was covering the fencing match, and hoped the pretrial publicity would influence the jury. It didn't. Hamlet's excuse to Laertes was "disingenuous" (Levin at 113). Hamlet's own expert, Samuel Johnson, admitted the "falsehood" of this apology on cross-examination and wished that "Hamlet had made some other defence." *The Plays of William Shakespeare* (1775) (vol. 8).

What we have said here applies equally well to Hamlet's effort to avoid responsibility under Penal Law § 125.25 (extreme emotional disturbance), an affirmative defense that the jury rejected and which is not satisfied by evidence of "stress." *People v. LaSalle*, 105 A.D.2d 756, 481 N.Y.S.2d 408 (2d Dept. 1984) (stress not amounting to loss of control inadequate). We discuss this issue further at Point III.

Appellant argues that he must be insane because he saw and conversed with the ghost of King Hamlet. This Court need not decide whether the ghost is real, although we can't help adding that three others also saw it, on three separate evenings, that they heard it order them to "swear" an oath, and that the ghost's specific information about King Hamlet's death turned out to be correct. Be that as it may, having seen and talked to the ghost, Hamlet rationally and, as his counsel admitted in summation, in a "lawyerly" fashion (Daniel Kornstein, *Kill All the Lawyers? Shakespeare's Legal Appeal* at 97), pursued "grounds / More relative than this" before murdering Claudius. Even on appeal, contradicting himself, the defendant takes "credit" for this caution, citing its "civilizing dimension," while also proclaiming his insanity. See Point VI infra.

II.

WHEN HAMLET KILLED LAERTES, HE WAS INCENSED
AND KNEW HE HAD AN UNBATED SWORD
CAPABLE OF INFLICTING A MORTAL WOUND

Although Laertes died as a result of the poison on his own sword, it was after Laertes had wounded Hamlet, thereby alerting Hamlet to the fact that Laertes's sword was "unbated." Hamlet could have retreated but instead, as John Dover Wilson told the jury, "he determines to get possession of" the unbated sword and did. (*What Happens In Hamlet* at 286.) Possessing this deadly weapon and "incensed" (5.2.305), Hamlet immediately invited Laertes to "come again" (5.2.306) and wounded him. Hamlet survived, of course, but had he retreated, as the law required (Penal Law § 35.15(2)(a)), Laertes would also have survived. That Laertes died of the poison and not of the mortal wound Hamlet intended is of no moment. *Matter of Anthony M,* 63 N.Y.2d 270, 280 (1984) (defendant's act need not be the "sole cause of death . . . other causes . . . will not relieve defendant of responsibility").

III.

HAMLET KILLED POLONIUS BELIEVING THAT POLONIUS
WAS THE KING AND WITH NO REASONABLE BELIEF
THAT HE OR THE QUEEN WERE IN DANGER

After killing Polonius, Hamlet asked: "Is it the King?" (3.4.27) and referring to the body added "I took thee for thy better" (3.4.33). A person who kills one person thinking he is another is guilty of murder. Penal Law § 125.25(1). Further, Hamlet did not "reasonably believ[e]" that either he or Gertrude were targets of "deadly physical force." Penal Law § 35.15(2)(a). Polonius's only utterance was a cry for "help," not a threat of harm. (3.4.24).

If extreme emotional disturbance were present, it would be here because Hamlet had just received confirmation of Claudius's guilt. But in the interval Hamlet encountered the king and made a calculated choice to await a more damning moment to get revenge. The lower Court gave Hamlet broad rein to show his emotional state, as was his burden. The jury found his proof wanting.

IV.

HAMLET'S MANSLAUGHTER CONVICTION FOR "RECKLESSLY" CAUSING OPHELIA'S DEATH SHOULD BE AFFIRMED

Ophelia did not reject Hamlet first. "[I]t is Hamlet who rejects Ophelia's love," Harold Jenkins told the jury. *Hamlet* (Arden Shakespeare ed.) at 150. Certainly, the sheltered young woman followed her father's instructions to return Hamlet's gifts, but in light of the ghost's information, Hamlet had already chosen to forsake Ophelia and women generally. The Nunnery scene revealed his growing disdain for women ("Wouldst thou be a breeder of sinners?") (3.1.122–23). He even treats Ophelia as "everywoman" when he tells her that "wise men know well enough what monsters *you* make of them." (3.1.140–41). And this: "God hath given *you* one face, and you make yourselves another." (3.1.145–46). (Emphases added.) Hamlet's abuse of Ophelia is calculated, not madness. He had just concluded a speech ("To be or not to be") asking, in exquisite poetry, fundamental questions about the condition of humankind.

Hamlet abused Ophelia further in the closet scene, where he pretended to be a distraught lover. As Professor A. C. Bradley testified, Hamlet's strategy was to demonstrate that "his sanity was not due to any mysterious unknown cause, but to his disappointment, and so to allay the suspicions of the king." (Shakespearean Tragedy at 155–56.) The defendant is a calculating man.

Having trifled with Ophelia's feelings ("I did love you once" and then "I loved you not") (3.1.116 and 120) in the Nunnery scene, and having subjected Ophelia to the humiliation of public rejection, Hamlet did not hesitate to abuse her again in the minutes before *The Murder of Gonzago* (*e.g.*, "Lady, shall I lie in your lap?") (3.2.110) when it served his purposes to do so. Ophelia was instantly receptive to this renewed interest but it, like the madness, was feigned for ulterior reasons.

Ophelia's subsequent death, whether or not suicide, was predictable. Hamlet took no steps to prevent it. He could have provided some system of support for this orphan—no mother, father slain, brother in Paris—but he did nothing, nor did he so much as acknowledge her plight until, ever competitive, Hamlet disrupted her funeral to show he could outmourn Laertes. ("I loved Ophelia. Forty thousand brothers / Could not with all their quality of love / Make up my sum.") (5.1.272–74).

The jury properly found that Hamlet "recklessly" caused Ophelia's death. Penal Law § 125.15(1). Alternatively, the State proved the lesser included offense of criminally negligent homicide (Penal Law § 125.10): Hamlet failed to "perceive a substantial and unjustifiable risk" of Ophelia's death resulting from conduct that "constitutes a gross deviation from the standard of care that a reasonable person would observe." Penal Law § 15.05(4).

V.

HAMLET IS SUBJECT TO THE JURISDICTION OF DENMARK
FOR THE DEATHS OF ROSENCRANTZ AND GUILDENSTERN
BECAUSE HE ACTED WHILE ON A DANISH VESSEL

Appellant cites the law of a state, not a nation, in making this jurisdictional argument. Denmark may validly assert jurisdiction when acts that cause death occur on a Danish vessel. See 18 U.S.C. § 7(1). Hamlet has not otherwise sought to excuse his conduct toward Rosencrantz and Guildenstern, but we take this opportunity to emphasize the cold-blooded nature of his scheme, whereby these schoolmates (unaware of the king's plot) would be instantly killed on arrival in England, "Not shriving-time allowed." (5.2.47).

Hamlet's loyal friend Horatio admitted on cross-examination that he had expressed shock at Hamlet's acts ("So Guildenstern and Rosencrantz go to 't") (5.2.56), a response that prompted Hamlet to his heartless admission: "Why, man, they did make love to this employment. / They are not near my conscience. . . ." (5.2.57–58).

Not near his conscience! The jury could properly have used this evidence to recognize Hamlet for what he is, a "proud, revengeful, ambitious" man, as he himself conceded (3.1.125–26), and a cold-blooded killer of all his victims. Bernard Grebanier, *The Heart of Hamlet* at 465 n.17 (equating Hamlet's indifference here with his lack of concern after he slew Polonius).

VI.

THIS COURT SHOULD NOT DISMISS THE INDICTMENT "IN THE INTEREST OF JUSTICE," FOR A SERIAL KILLER WHO SHOWS NO CONTRITION

What we have so far shown amply demonstrates how monstrous it would be for this Court to relieve the defendant of his criminal responsibility in the interest of justice. We pause only to note the blatant contradiction between Hamlet's assertion under this Point—that his "delay does him credit" and "reflects [the] civilizing function of law"—with his earlier argument that he was suffering from a "mental disease or defect" that rendered him unable to know that his acts were wrong.

Hamlet's "interest of justice" defense is the only nonjurisdictional defense he offers for his murder of Claudius. Yet when Hamlet slew Claudius, with a "point" he knew was "envenomed" (5.2.324), he could safely have retreated and won vindication in law. He had proof of Claudius's scheme on his own life—the king's letter to the English monarch. Because, as next explained, Denmark is an elective monarchy, this letter could have been used to depose Claudius. Hamlet may or may not have been able to convince a law court that Claudius killed his father, based on the demeanor evidence at *The Murder of Gonzago,* but Laertes's dying declaration, Fed.R.Ev. 804(b)(2) (5.2.316–23), together with the physical evidence, would have established Claudius's legal guilt for the death of Gertrude.

VII.

HAMLET ENJOYS NO IMMUNITY AS SOVEREIGN BECAUSE FORTINBRAS, NOT HAMLET, IS MONARCH

Hamlet is not the Danish monarch. The Danish monarch is elected. As Mr. Jenkins testified, Claudius became king "with public consent" and then "consolidated his position by a prudent marriage" to Gertrude. *Hamlet (Arden Shakespeare,* ed.) at 433–34. The current king is Fortinbras, elected after Hamlet slew Claudius. The councilors rejected Hamlet for the obvious reason that he should not be allowed to profit from a homicidal act. On conviction, they also stripped Hamlet of his title and struck his name from the roll of student attorneys. Whatever may have been the practice in England under Lear, Denmark has an elected monarchy. *Id.* Further, no sovereign immunity attaches to a criminal act committed before occupying the royal office. Otherwise a reigning monarch could be "legally" murdered by the next in succession, or that monarch and the next in succession could both be "legally" murdered by the second in succession, and so on. This is not law.

We do not doubt that Hamlet wanted the crown ("He that hath . . . / Popped in between th' election and my hopes") (5.2.65.). But Claudius, not Hamlet, was elected king and on his death Fortinbras, not Hamlet, was asked to reign.

Hamlet is not king. Hamlet is a convicted serial murderer.

CONCLUSION

The defendant's homicides have resulted in the deaths of six people, including an entire family of three. The convictions should be affirmed.

Respectfully submitted,

STEPHEN GILLERS
Attorney for Appellee

Of counsel: Hayley Baruk, Davida H. Isaacs, Christopher M. Locke, Linda A. Shashoua, Jonathan Wayne (admitted under the Elsinore Student Practice Rule)

ROYAL DANISH COURT OF APPEALS

FOR THE ELSINORE CIRCUIT

———————

STATE OF DENMARK,

APPELLEE,

against

HAMLET, PRINCE (AND FUTURE KING) OF DENMARK,

APPELLANT

APPELLANT'S REPLY BRIEF

DANIEL J. KORNSTEIN

Attorney for Appellant

The government's brief is full of legalistic "quiddits" (*i.e.*, subtleties) and "quillets" (*i.e.*, evasions) (5.1.99–100). It has the novel, odd, and revisionist distinction of quickly dispatching one of the greatest heroes in Western civilization, a most thoughtful figure, an "idealist" with exquisite "moral" sensibility (A. C. Bradley, *Shakespearean Tragedy* 111–13 (Penguin 1991)), as no more than a remorseless, psychopathic "serial killer." The government's brief equates appellant with Ted Bundy. But the equation is false, the government's quillets easily exposed, and a sinister abuse of legal process unmasked.

Quillet No. 1: Although the government scoffs at appellant's argument based on lack of mental capacity, Hamlet's "madness is surely the most interesting and most challenging" aspect of this case, as one expert testified. K. R. Eissler, *Discourse on Hamlet and HAMLET* 400 (1971). But expert testimony can be found to support either side of the question. An expert cited by the government has testified, "Hamlet's state of mind is one of those questions upon which all of the doctors have disagreed." Harry Levin, *The Question of Hamlet* 111 (1959).

The record itself, rather than the divided experts' testimony, is a better guide. While stressing appellant's sometimes pretended madness, the government turns a blind eye to all proof of Hamlet's genuine emotional disturbance. The evidence will simply not support a finding that appellant was *always* faking his unbalanced mental state. Nor does it help the government to imply that talking ghosts, like UFOs, are real if seen by more than one person. The government ignores the dual character of appellant's madness, one part feigned, one part real.

What the government sarcastically dubs the "Abused Prince Syndrome" was a mental condition no different from the battered-wife syndrome, post-traumatic stress disorder, or the child-abuse accommodation syndrome in that, in conjunction with mental illness, it gave rise to terrible acts of violence for which Hamlet was not responsible.

Quillet No. 2: As to Laertes's death, the government here slides over the crucial facts: Laertes conspired with Claudius to challenge Hamlet to a fencing match in which Laertes would use a poisoned sword to kill Hamlet even with a slight scratch, and then Laertes carried out those murderous plans (4.7.124–63). Contrary to the sly innuendoes of the government's brief, Hamlet wounded Laertes with the poisoned sword *before* Laertes told him it was poisoned, and *before* Laertes confessed and implicated Claudius (5.2.316–23). This was, after all, an athletic contest, a fencing match in which the fencers are not supposed to retreat but to attack, and in which injuries are expected to occur. The law did not require appellant to retreat in these circumstances, especially since he did not know the sword he held was tipped with poison. And since he did not know of the poisoned tip, he lacked *mens rea* and cannot be charged with the consequences of that poison.

Quillet No. 3: The government wrongly mocks appellant's defense of justification regarding Polonius's death. In addition to the justifiable use of force in the circumstances, to be found—as Polonius was—in a queen's bedroom has long been regarded as the capital crime of treason. *See* Thomas Malory, *Le Morte d'Arthur* (1485).

Quillet No. 4: The government's fine-spun attempt to hold Hamlet criminally liable for Ophelia's death is without support in fact or law. The government misstates the record by baldly asserting that "Ophelia did not reject Hamlet first." *Govt. Br.* 4. The facts are otherwise. *Before* Hamlet ever said anything unpleasant to Ophelia, she obeyed her father and brother, and "did repel" Hamlet's "letters and denied / His access to me." (2.1.111–12). The comments relied on by the government occurred *after* Ophelia, whatever her inner feelings, outwardly rejected Hamlet. The law cannot expect Hamlet to divine Ophelia's interior thoughts and feelings if they are at odds with her behavior.

On the law, the government's position is equally untenable. Lovers will have occasional quarrels, say things in the heat of the moment, and will even break up. It would violate public policy—rooted in common sense and human experience—to impose criminal liability on one lover for the emotional consequences of breaking up with the other lover. A failed romance is one of life's risks, otherwise relationships would be held hostage to threats of suicide.

Quillet No. 5: There is no evidence in the record that the "bark" transporting Hamlet and his false friends Rosencrantz and Guildenstern to England was a Danish vessel, as the government asserts (4.3.41–47). The vessel could as easily have been an English one making a return trip, or for that matter a ship flying a Dutch or French flag. Thus, the government has failed to carry its burden of proof on the issue of jurisdiction here.

Quillet No. 6: The government's opposition to dismissal "in the interest of justice" should shock the Court's conscience. As one expert testified, "Nearly all readers, commentators, and critics are agreed in thinking that it was Hamlet's duty to kill." Harold Goddard, *The Meaning of Shakespeare* 333 (1951). Indeed, two of the government's own experts—A. C. Bradley and John Dover Wilson—testified that Hamlet had such a "sacred duty." It is paradoxical to punish someone for carrying out what "nearly all" think was a sacred duty.

Quillet No. 7: In arguing against sovereign immunity for Prince (soon-to-be king) Hamlet, the government, run by Fortinbras's foreign cronies, not surprisingly misunderstands the Danish constitution. Denmark is no elective monarchy; Hamlet is its rightful king. Claudius publicly declared Hamlet to be his royal heir: "[T]hink of us / As a father; for let the world take note, / You are the most immediate to our throne" (1.2.107–09). And Rosencrantz told Hamlet, "[Y]ou have the voice of the king himself for your succession in Denmark" (3.2.339–40). Polonius also views Hamlet as Claudius's successor (1.3.20–24).

Fortinbras is not the real king of Denmark. When he mistakenly thought he was dying, Hamlet said Fortinbras, in the power vacuum, would be king. (5.2.356–58) But Hamlet lives and he, not the foreign invader Fortinbras, is the true Danish sovereign. Fortinbras has conceded Hamlet's claim to the Danish throne, admitting that Hamlet, if he lived, would "have proved most royal" (5.2.390, 399–400). And so he shall.

CONCLUSION

The government's argument against sovereign immunity unwittingly reveals the sinister motive behind this prosecution. It is a common story of the corrupting influence of power. Fortinbras, having seized the throne in Denmark without any lawful claim, now refuses to step down. His attorney general seeks to keep Prince Hamlet, Fortinbras's only rival, in prison for life because Hamlet is "loved" by the "multitude" (4.3.4 and 4.7.19) and poses a genuine threat to Fortinbras's naked power grab. *Cf.* Richard III and the Princes in the Tower; Elizabeth I and Mary Queen of Scots.

We appeal to the integrity and the independence of this Court not to be cowed by the trappings of authority as represented by the illegal Fortinbras regime, but to do the right thing. *Cf. United States v. Nixon,* 418 U.S. 683 (1974); *N.Y. Times Co. v. United States,* 403 U.S. 713 (1971).

For the reasons given, the conviction below should be reversed.

Respectfully submitted,

DANIEL J. KORNSTEIN
Attorney for Appellant

27

THE ELSINORE APPEAL

People

v.

Hamlet

AT THE ASSOCIATION OF THE BAR

OF THE CITY OF NEW YORK

OCTOBER 11, 1994

NORMAN GREENE: My name is Norman Greene, and I am Chair of the Committee on Lectures and Continuing Education at the Association of the Bar of the City of New York, the Committee that has brought you this program. This program is based on Shakespeare's *Hamlet,* with one exception: Hamlet survived and lived to be tried. Can you imagine what would have happened if this had occurred today? It certainly would have eclipsed the O.J. Simpson trial.

So let me introduce the cast and give the credits. The program subcommittee responsible for putting it together is chaired by Ellen Simon, working with Eliot P. Green, Philip T. Temple, Stephen F. Selig and L. Priscilla Hall. Without them, without Ellen and the subcommittee, nothing would have happened here at all.

We have a three-judge panel tonight. Our presiding judge is not a judge at all, but a Shakespearean scholar. This is most appropriate. She is Professor Jeanne Roberts, professor of literature at American University in Washington, D.C. Professor Roberts is a former President of the Shakespeare Association of America and author most recently of *The Shakespearean Wild: Geography, Genus, and Gender.* She is also one of the authors of a book called *Shakespeare Set Free* on the teaching of *Hamlet* and *Henry IV: Part I.* Our other judges are well known for being judges. Most of you know Judge Kevin Duffy of the United States District Court for the Southern District of New York. He was most recently in the news for the World Trade Center bombing case. Also, former U.S. District Judge Marvin Frankel, who is now a partner at the Kramer, Levin, Naftalis, Nessen, Kamin & Frankel firm. Our advocates are Daniel Kornstein and Professor Stephen Gillers of New York University School of Law. Professor Gillers is a specialist in the regulation of lawyers and the author of a casebook on the subject. Whenever you see anybody asked anything about legal ethics, Professor Gillers is generally the one to be quoted. Dan Kornstein is the author of a new book on Shakespeare and the Law entitled: *Kill All the Lawyers: Shakespeare's Legal Appeal.* Dan is a partner at Kornstein, Veisz & Wexler.

In case you may have wondered, this Shakespeare program was born when I happened to call Dan about things our committee might do, and he told me that he was just completing a book on Shakespeare. One thing led to another, and here we are tonight. Dan is representing Hamlet; representing the people is Professor Gillers.

Finally, let me address a question you may have thought of. What is the Association doing with matters like this? Why are we doing a Shakespeare program? Perhaps those of you who were at our trial of Thomas Jefferson last June presided over by Chief Justice Rehnquist may have the answer. In devising our programs, the Committee on Lectures and Continuing Education tries to dream and imagine what can be done even if never done or thought of before. We do not have to do programs limited to new developments in Section 105 of some statute. We also have a special affinity to literary and historical subjects.

Finally one last announcement. The briefs on appeal are on the back table. If you missed them and do not have a copy, *The New York Law Journal* was kind enough to publish them in full on Friday and today. How many times have you seen briefs in real cases published? Here they published, in full, briefs in a made-up case.

Professor Roberts will begin tonight's appeal. I will turn this over to her at this point.

PROFESSOR ROBERTS: I would guess that we could make a bet that there is no one in this room that doesn't know what happens in *Hamlet.* However, I have been asked to give you a brief summary. This is slightly shorter than the skinhead *Hamlet,* but the vocabulary is slightly larger. The main reason I'm bothering with this actually is that I think chronology may have some bearing on the way we come out in the end. Okay. Hold on to your seatbelts.

Hamlet returns from Wittenberg for his father's funeral and his mother's marriage. Marcellus, Bernardo, and Horatio see the ghost of Hamlet's father on the ramparts. Hamlet sees the ghost somewhat later and resolves to test what the ghost has told him, namely that his father was killed by his uncle by pouring poison in his ears while he was sleeping in the garden. Laertes, the son of the counselor to the king, Polonius, asks leave to return to France and warns his sister Ophelia, that Hamlet probably can't, and won't, marry her. Polonius has his famous advice to Laertes; the most famous part of it is of course ". . . Neither a borrower nor a lender be." And he says good-bye to Laertes, and Laertes goes off to Paris.

Ophelia reports that Hamlet has appeared to her in her closet, apparently mad, looking very undressed with his stockings hanging down and so on. But they don't know why. Polonius reports to the king that Hamlet is mad with love. The king sets Rosencrantz and Guildenstern, two friends of Hamlet from Wittenberg, to try to find out what's going on with Hamlet. Fortinbras, a Norwegian prince, gets permission to pass through Denmark, on his way to fight another battle. The king and the queen read Hamlet's love letters to Ophelia and entertain the idea that maybe this is why Hamlet is mad. Hamlet spends a lot of time baiting Polonius and Rosencrantz and Guildenstern; lots of funny scenes where he's making fun of them. Polonius and Rosencrantz and Guildenstern announce that the players are coming, and this gives Hamlet the brilliant idea that he will test his uncle, by putting on a recapitulation of the murder of his father, which he does. He gets the players to help him.

Polonius and the king decide that they're going to

eavesdrop on an interview between Ophelia and Hamlet in order to find out whether Hamlet is really mad for love, and they do that. Hamlet comes in and gives Ophelia that terrible speech ". . . Get thee to a nunnery. Do not be a breeder of sinners" and so on. The king after listening to that says it's not love. Then they have the play. They go through it twice. The second time the king rushes out saying, "Give me some light." And this is taken by Hamlet to be an admission of guilt. The next thing we see, the king is praying in his chamber. We still don't know for sure whether the king is guilty until we hear his prayer. But Hamlet decides not to kill him at that point because he's afraid he will go to heaven if killed while praying.

Hamlet then goes to see his mother in her closet to tell her to stay away from Claudius. And Polonius hides behind the curtain in order to overhear. At one point the queen thinks she is about to be murdered. She's very upset and she says, "Will you murder me?" Polonius at that point cries, "Help! Ho!" and Hamlet kills him thinking he is the king. The ghost appears briefly but only to Hamlet. Hamlet tells Gertrude that he is not mad. Claudius plans to send Hamlet to England with Rosencrantz and Guildenstern, and he has privately sent, with them, a letter asking the king of England to kill Hamlet when he arrives.

Ophelia comes in mad, presumably over grief that her father is dead. Horatio gets a letter that Hamlet has miraculously been taken off the ship to England, being saved by pirates, and the king discovers that Hamlet is back and so he's got to deal with him again. He thought he got rid of him but he didn't. Ophelia has meanwhile drowned by accident or suicide. The king plots with Laertes who has now found out that his sister is dead. They plot that they will have a duel; that Hamlet will have a bated sword but Laertes will have an unbated sword and it will also be poisoned. The king is going to have a poison cup just in case none of the other things work.

They do fight. Hamlet is wounded by Laertes. He wounds Laertes in return by taking up the poisoned sword. Laertes dies. Hamlet, in what we thought was going to be his dying moment, says, "The election lights on Fortinbras." But, of course, Hamlet doesn't die so we now have those questions open, and I think we are perhaps ready then to hear from Mr. Kornstein.

MR. KORNSTEIN. Thank you, Your Honor. May it please the court, just before Hamlet thought he was going to die he said to his friend Horatio, "Tell my story. Report me and my cause aright." Now Horatio wasn't a lawyer; he couldn't come here and do what Hamlet wanted him to do. Hamlet also told him, "What a wounded name, things standing thus unknown shall live behind me." Depending on what happens here will determine whether or not Hamlet was prophetic. Horatio then says, "Let me speak to the yet unknowing world how these things came about." And that we will do.

The trial below, indeed this entire case, is a political trial. Fortinbras, this Norwegian invader, has stolen the throne from Hamlet and now tries to keep his chief rival, beloved by the multitude, in prison for life. It's a common tale. We've seen it many times in history. But this court has the power to set it right.

Fortinbras has no claim to be king. He simply stepped into a power vacuum. And remember just before Laertes died, and there are many witnesses to this, when Laertes makes his confession, he says the king is to blame and explains how Claudius, that other usurper, was responsible for all the evil that happened. Now the king's to blame a second time over. The first time it was King Claudius, this time the king to blame is king Fortinbras for pursuing this trial and for keeping Hamlet in prison.

JUDGE FRANKEL: Mr. Kornstein, you mention Hamlet's being in prison for life. I don't think the record makes it clear and I wonder if you could tell us. Is he on bail?

MR. KORNSTEIN: No, Your Honor. No, Your Honor. He has been rotting in prison for these 400 years.

JUDGE FRANKEL: But he's all right.

MR. KORNSTEIN: So far as we know. And, to turn it even further, when appellant made one of his more famous speeches, and there were some people overhearing it, again he talks about, ". . . to be or not to be" (his suicidal impulses); he talks about the "oppressor's wrong"; "the proud man's contumely"; "the law's delay" (and the four hundred years qualifies), and the "insolence of office." That's what we have with king Fortinbras and the attorney general who's trying to keep Hamlet in jail. Hamlet was prophetic. But perhaps we can clear away some of the underbrush and get to what we think are some of the easier charges.

There are six homicides that are involved in this case on this appeal. Five of them are for second-degree murder: Rosencrantz, Guildenstern, Claudius, Laertes, Polonius. Ophelia is for second-degree manslaughter. Let's start with Ophelia because it really is the easiest case. Even on the chief judge's recitation of the facts, if Ophelia committed suicide because of her father's death . . .

PROFESSOR ROBERTS: Excuse me for interrupting, but why do you think she committed suicide? We have what seems to be an eyewitness account that she slipped, held on to a willow, fell into the brook and drowned. She didn't jump in the brook.

MR. KORNSTEIN: Your Honor, then we can make a motion to dismiss right now. If the court is willing to agree, then we'll just pass over Ophelia and have an acquittal.

PROFESSOR ROBERTS: It seems to me you overlooked something that might help your case.

MR. KORNSTEIN: There's also the conversation during the funeral between the priest and the people that she's not entitled to the full rights of burial because her death was in doubt.

PROFESSOR ROBERTS: She's buried in consecrated ground and she does have some funeral rites.

MR. KORNSTEIN: But not all.

PROFESSOR ROBERTS: Not all. Right.

MR. KORNSTEIN: But if, okay, we can have a continuum. If she slipped and fell, Hamlet—not guilty. Conviction reversed. If it was because of her grief over Polonius's death, again, that's not something to make Hamlet criminally liable for. And even, worst case, is if it was because Hamlet broke her heart. The facts show that she dumped Hamlet, at least by outward appearances, first. She was the one who listened to her father and her brother, and refused to see Hamlet.

JUDGE DUFFY: But didn't she, or wasn't she turned off by Hamlet's madness? And why are you abandoning the idea of diminished capability or mental capacity?

MR. KORNSTEIN: Your Honor, we abandon nothing. That's a significant part of the appeal. The diminished capacity argument cuts across the board but, starting with the easier arguments first. . . .

JUDGE FRANKEL: How easy is it if he deliberately drove her to commit suicide?

MR. KORNSTEIN: But that's a conclusion, Your Honor. What did he do? At worst he said some things to her—after she had stopped accepting his advances—said some things that may have been cruel, may have been nasty. But human experience teaches us that happens when someone has a failed romance.

JUDGE FRANKEL: What about when he's expecting to see her and he's pretending to talk to himself. He could be heard in the balcony of the theater, in spite of his pretense. And he's extolling the virtues of suicide with this young woman. You don't think that was part of a calculated plot to lead her to her undoing?

MR. KORNSTEIN: Absolutely not. There's never been a suggestion in the text or in any of the expert witnesses that Hamlet intended to compel, or to assist, or to drive Ophelia to commit suicide. As he says later, and as the play bears out, he did love her. What Your Honor refers to was part of his feigned madness. His object was Claudius and the people around Claudius, to try and offset their view of what was really going on in his mind.

JUDGE DUFFY: Do we get back to your suggestion that the madness was feigned, and at the same time you suggest that he had a diminished mental capacity that was unfeigned?

MR. KORNSTEIN: At times. Let's go to that then, now. Hamlet did fake being mad at times, at other times he was not faking, and we can break those times into portions in the play. In the first act, before anything about an "antic disposition" goes on, Horatio says that Hamlet is acting weird, that Hamlet "Waxes with desperate imagination." And he warns Hamlet that the ghost may take away his sovereign reason and drive him to madness. It's only *after* that Hamlet comes up with the plan that he'll pretend at some times to be sick. But let's look at the actual situation, about which there is no dispute. Young man somewhere: He's a student at school; around twenty. His father dies. Within a very short period of time, his mother marries his uncle. He learns from a ghost (and let's talk about delusional behavior there: he learns from a ghost who tells him to kill his uncle and seek revenge, right?) that something's wrong, that these things happened. Denmark, all of Scandinavia, is known for its high suicide rate. Another lawyer in town might call it Danish rage.

But there is a reality as well. In the famous scene, where Hamlet confronts his mother Gertrude in her bedroom, with Polonius watching from, listening from behind the curtains, he tells her he's not mad, he's not crazy and he's going to hold up a mirror to her face so she can see what she herself really has done. And yet when the ghost appears, then, no one else can see the ghost. And one of the points the attorney general makes is that several other people—three other people— saw the ghost, as if the number of people who see UFOs make them real. But in that scene with Gertrude, Gertrude didn't see the ghost, and as Hamlet is talking to the ghost, Gertrude says, "You are having discourse with the incorporal air." Now, it's in that scene when he gets overwrought. He is confronting his mother. He wants her to stay. She gets worried. She thinks he's going to lose control and perhaps hurt her. She screams for help. That's when Polonius yells for help. Hamlet wheels around in the heat of the moment, tremendously upset. And that's the first death, not counting his father's death.

JUDGE DUFFY: You convinced me he was excited, but not nuts.

MR. KORNSTEIN: Well, the law has different levels. Let's talk about the lower one of extreme emotional disturbance. I think it's impossible to look at the record and say that Hamlet was not extremely disturbed by the events that were going on in his life. It was more than just a little bit of stress. He was extremely emotionally disturbed and from his point of view, he had good reason. I mean, talk about a dysfunctional family. There were some things going on there.

PROFESSOR ROBERTS: Would you mind telling me why you think he had a dysfunctional family? He seems to have had a happily married mother and father. His mother loved him. His father loved him.

MR. KORNSTEIN: I'm not sure how you can say that. There's some suggestion that before Hamlet Sr. was done away with, that perhaps his mother, Hamlet's mother, and Claudius the uncle were involved with each other.

PROFESSOR ROBERTS: Where do you find that suggestion?

MR. KORNSTEIN: By the quickness of time to the marriage. That's an inference, not proof; that's circumstantial.

PROFESSOR ROBERTS: Yeah, let me ask you one other question. How old do you think Hamlet was when his father died?

MR. KORNSTEIN: Approximately twenty.

PROFESSOR ROBERTS: The text tells us that he was at least thirty. It's a little hard to think of him as an abused son.

MR. KORNSTEIN: Well, it may show that he was learning disabled if he was still in school.

PROFESSOR ROBERTS: It just shows that he was studying law.

MR. KORNSTEIN: And it may be that the witness who testified to his being so was incorrect. Either way, I don't think it changes the central thrust for all of us. Death of a parent is a grievous moment. And if it's under suspicious circumstances that may turn out to be the murder by another family member and then the quick or hasty marriage of the surviving parent, certainly we can all empathize with Hamlet's feelings.

JUDGE FRANKEL: Mr. Kornstein, you rely on Hamlet's own testimony that he was crazy, to prove he was crazy. Is that good law? Is he an expert in this subject?

MR. KORNSTEIN: Crazy is not a word I would use, Your Honor.

JUDGE FRANKEL: Mad?

MR. KORNSTEIN: I wouldn't use those words. That's not what the law says. I think that his testimony is helpful on whether he understood the difference from right or wrong in his actions, because certainly every time he did something that he is accused of doing he thought what he was doing was right, and everybody around him (and the press coverage since these events) has criticized him for not killing Claudius much sooner.

JUDGE FRANKEL: But I'm looking at page two [page 4] of your brief. And I'm reading the testimony. "I here proclaim was

40

madness. Was't Hamlet wronged Laertes? Never Hamlet . . .
His madness is poor Hamlet's enemy." If I understand your
brief, you rely on that as some evidence that he was suffering
from madness. Do you not?

MR. KORNSTEIN: I rely on it for some evidence. There was much
expert testimony below, Your Honor, but, as has to be frankly
admitted, the experts divided. There is no consensus as to
whether Hamlet was or was not mad, according to the
experts. So when the experts divide, I think it's appropriate to
look to other sources of information. Other evidence, and
certainly direct testimony from the defendant, as well as
other people, would be helpful.

JUDGE FRANKEL: And that's testimony to his madness, and you're
saying he's a competent witness to testify to that. I notice
that you rely on Sam Johnson as well and I believe you'd
agree he was also crazy. I mean, how many nuts do you have
that you're invoking in order to overturn this jury verdict?

MR. KORNSTEIN: Your Honor, the question we have is what do we
do when expert testimony divides? The state saw fit to try
Hamlet, which means the state, the "rotten" state, has
determined that Hamlet now is mentally competent.
Therefore, he can testify. Otherwise he shouldn't have been
tried. And he'd probably been out 375 years ago. So yes, we
do rely on his testimony as well as all the other witnesses as
to what happened, what he said and the acts that went on.
What we have to distinguish is when Hamlet was faking it
and when it was real. And that's something that usually is
obvious from the context. When he's around Polonius, he's
faking it. When he's around Claudius, he's faking it except
when Claudius can't hear him. Remember when Claudius
was praying and Hamlet is thinking about killing him but

decides not to. Hamlet's not faking anything then. When Hamlet's with his mother, he's not faking anything. When Hamlet's with Rosencrantz and Guildenstern, most of the time he's faking it. Not always.

PROFESSOR ROBERTS: It seems to me you're on really shaky ground when you try to argue that his scenes with anybody reveal, ultimately, his state of mind. The things that do seem to me to reveal his state of mind are when he's talking to himself. And when he's talking to himself, which he does at greater length than any other character in the play, there's no madness.

MR. KORNSTEIN: Your Honor, I would say talking at length to one's self is pretty good evidence . . .

PROFESSOR ROBERTS: Talking to yourself in a room full of people is somewhat different. I'm a little disturbed by you even talking about his committing suicide. That's not what he says. He says, "'tis nobler in the mind to suffer / The slings and arrows of outrageous fortune, / Or to take arms against a sea of troubles / And by opposing, end them?" [3.1.58–61]. That's the choice.

MR. KORNSTEIN: He says some other things, too, Your Honor.

PROFESSOR ROBERTS: He never says he's thinking of killing himself.

MR. KORNSTEIN: When he and Polonius are having a conversation . . .

PROFESSOR ROBERTS: We know we can't trust that.

MR. KORNSTEIN: But you said . . . it's some evidence of something.

PROFESSOR ROBERTS: Okay. What?

MR. KORNSTEIN: Polonius says, "What could I take from you?" And Hamlet says, only my life. That's some indication that he's thinking about suicide. And certainly the beginning of the speech that you were talking about, "To be or not to be . . ." certainly has come down to us as having something to do with thoughts about suicide, which would not be out of place in his situation.

PROFESSOR ROBERTS: Well, I didn't want to slow you up forever but I do think that that's not proof that he's thinking about suicide. He's thinking of whether he should do something or not do something.

MR. KORNSTEIN: The fact that someone is even contemplating the subject means that the thought has crossed his mind.

PROFESSOR ROBERTS: He's not contemplating the subject of suicide.

JUDGE DUFFY: Is he not contemplating whether he is to fulfill his destiny as he sees it?

MR. KORNSTEIN: There's a whole patch in the speech about "to sleep perchance to dream" and to go to "the country from which no one ever returns." There's certainly a theme that he's considering doing away with his life as a way of escaping his earthly and worldly troubles. That's not something I'm making up.

JUDGE FRANKEL: Do you rely on the insanity defense against the charge of murdering Claudius?

MR. KORNSTEIN: Among other things.

JUDGE FRANKEL: Among other things?

MR. KORNSTEIN: Among other things. Absolutely.

JUDGE FRANKEL: Are you then urging that if he had been sane he wouldn't have killed Claudius?

MR. KORNSTEIN: I don't understand Your Honor.

JUDGE FRANKEL: I'll say it again. Are you urging that, but for his insanity he would not have killed Claudius?

MR. KORNSTEIN: If this were at a trial, I'd say that's an objectionable question because it's a "what if" question, and we don't know. We don't know what he would have done if he didn't do what he did.

JUDGE FRANKEL: Overruled. Objection overruled.

JUDGE DUFFY: I haven't forgotten.

MR. KORNSTEIN: The question is that if he had no diminished mental capacity . . .

JUDGE FRANKEL: Are you arguing that if he had not been insane he would not have killed Claudius? 'Cause if you're not, I don't know what your insanity defense means with respect to Claudius.

MR. KORNSTEIN: The question . . . the reason why it's objectionable is because it's unanswerable. All right? We don't know what he would've done if he were not insane or temporarily insane, since that's what he was.

JUDGE FRANKEL: Well don't you say in his brief that he had a sacred duty to kill Claudius?

MR. KORNSTEIN: That's what everybody else thought.

JUDGE FRANKEL: What do you say?

MR. KORNSTEIN: I think that as the heir to the throne faced with the usurper, regicide, and the man who killed his father, that he may have had a sacred (whether it was a legal duty may be another matter) duty, but he may have had a sacred duty to avenge that death and then in the context of how that death occurred—in those last few moments after Claudius had just poisoned Hamlet's mother with the chalice full of the poisoned wine that was meant for Hamlet and after Hamlet had discovered Claudius's treachery with the envenomed and unbated sword for Laertes—that Hamlet would've had pretty good reason to be upset and angry.

JUDGE FRANKEL: You say he should be praised not punished.

MR. KORNSTEIN: Absolutely. I think the wrong person was in the dock in this trial.

JUDGE FRANKEL: But if you're claiming he was insane why should he be praised for something he did if he was off his head?

MR. KORNSTEIN: Well, he was temporarily insane. He wasn't insane all the time. And one can plead in the alternative, especially one faced with six homicide convictions.

If we could move on to one of the other issues: Rosencrantz and Guildenstern. Now those are nice friends for you. False friends if there ever were. They come back; they're called back by Claudius and they're accompanying Hamlet to England where he's going to be murdered. Claudius writes a letter to the English king: "Kill Hamlet immediately." What does Hamlet do? On the boat ride, he discovers the packet, keeps the packet with that letter, writes his own letter, forges a letter from Claudius to have Rosencrantz and Guildenstern killed by the English king. This happens on the ship, on the high seas. I say that there's no jurisdiction; that the government has failed to meet its burden of proof to show jurisdiction to this court. First, it didn't happen in Denmark. Secondly, there's no proof in the record that it was a Danish vessel. It could have been an English vessel going back . . .

JUDGE DUFFY: There's no proof there was not a Danish vessel either.

MR. KORNSTEIN: But it's the government's burden of proof. And since the government hasn't proved that it was a Danish vessel . . . dismissal. So having disposed of Rosencrantz and Guildenstern, we can move right along to Laertes.

JUDGE DUFFY: Was he crazy at the time or mad or . . .

MR. KORNSTEIN: Crazy like a fox.

JUDGE DUFFY: Oh! So he intended to get rid of the two of them.

MR. KORNSTEIN: Absolutely.

PROFESSOR ROBERTS: Let me ask you one other thing. All Hamlet did on the boat was write a letter saying kill Rosencrantz and Guildenstern. They were not killed until they got to England. So who has the legal, this is really for elucidation, who has the legal jurisdiction over the . . .

MR. KORNSTEIN: I would say nobody. I think he goes free. I mean under the circumstances, one might even argue a stretched self-defense argument.

JUDGE DUFFY: Well, it leaves two jurisdictions open for prosecution: England, where they would hang him all right; and, of course, the court of King Neptune, where he would be food for the fishes.

MR. KORNSTEIN: But England is an enlightened place, and while the punishment might be hanging, they wouldn't find him guilty.

JUDGE DUFFY: No. I see.

PROFESSOR ROBERTS: May I say one word in defense of Rosencrantz and Guildenstern? They were innocent bystanders. They did not know what was in that letter. They had never done anything to Hamlet except be a little bit stupid, and if we kill off all the stupid people in the world we're in trouble.

JUDGE DUFFY: No, but we'd be lonely.

PROFESSOR ROBERTS: Ah, well said.

MR. KORNSTEIN: Your Honor, I'm not sure that we can say that. How do we know that Rosencrantz and Guildenstern didn't know what was in that letter?

PROFESSOR ROBERTS: There's no indication that they did.

MR. KORNSTEIN: And vice versa. And certainly in the docudramas that have been put out on these events over the years, Rosencrantz and Guildenstern have been portrayed as sly and knowing individuals. And Tom Stoppard's docudrama of what happened after. . . . But let's go to Laertes. Look at what this fellow does. Laertes and Claudius hatch this plan. They're going to get Hamlet one way or another. If the poisoned unbated sword doesn't work, they're going to get him with the poisoned wine. All right? So they challenge him to a fencing match. Hamlet begs forgiveness of Laertes just before the match saying, "Look it wasn't me. I'm sorry. Please." And Laertes says, "I accept it in love but not in honor. We have to go through with this fencing match." Hamlet doesn't know it's a duel to the death. Hamlet thinks it's just a little sport. There's a wager on the outcome. What happens?

Hamlet surprises everybody. He gets the first two hits. Then, and here the testimony gets a little murky, but it's clear from the record that while Hamlet is unawares, and the docudramas usually portray Hamlet turning around going to his seconds, Laertes, this nice up-standing fellow, comes over and wounds him with the poisoned sword. Only Hamlet doesn't know it's poisoned. Hamlet feels himself being cut, gets angry because he feels he was taken advantage of, because he wasn't ready. It's like hitting a boxer while the boxer is in the corner. Hamlet turns around. There's a scuffle. They exchange swords, and Hamlet wounds Laertes, again, not knowing anything about the poison. It's only after that, that Laertes makes his confession. He explains that the sword was poisoned, they're both going to die momentarily (at least that's what they thought) and, and that Claudius was in on everything. All right. Now, how is Hamlet responsible for this? What was he supposed to do in a fencing match where he didn't know anything was poisoned? Run away? He's not supposed to retreat. He's supposed to fence. And if he doesn't know the point is poisoned, what criminal intention did he have?

JUDGE DUFFY: Does fencing include wounding?

MR. KORNSTEIN: Your Honor, in Heidelberg, there's a long tradition of duelling and a lot of scarred faces that are part of the process. Now, Hamlet had been studying in a German university, so it's part of the cultural tradition.

JUDGE FRANKEL: Is it clear Laertes is dead, by the way?

MR. KORNSTEIN: It had been clear for 400 years up until this moment.

JUDGE FRANKEL: Is this argument casting some doubt on it?

MR. KORNSTEIN: Your Honor, all the more reason perhaps for retrial if Laertes, it turns out, has not died. He may have some significant testimony.

JUDGE FRANKEL: I'm joining the Chief in helping you in the view that—although you don't need any help we should help you anyhow—if he's not dead, that would constitute a ground for acquittal, yes?

MR. KORNSTEIN: Certainly on a conviction for homicide.

JUDGE FRANKEL: What's your position on that? Is he dead?

MR. KORNSTEIN: I'll take the cue, no.

PROFESSOR ROBERTS: Do you think Hamlet was insane when he says, over the body of Polonius, first of all, "Thou wretched, rash, intruding fool, farewell! I took thee for thy better." [3.4.32–33]. And when he says a little bit later, "I'll lug the guts into the neighbor room." Is that insanity?

MR. KORNSTEIN: No.

PROFESSOR ROBERTS: Then what is it?

MR. KORNSTEIN: A reaction to an event that he did not intend. . . . He did not intend to kill Polonius. It was in the heat of the moment. He did not know who was behind that curtain, and keep in mind that there have been murders in that, or a murder of the king in that castle. They were in the queen's bedroom. There have been some societies that have viewed anybody being in the queen's bedroom as committing high treason. He didn't know what was happening. Now, is that insanity, his comments? What do they mean? I'm not sure what they mean except the reaction to a dead body that he was in some sense an agent in creating.

PROFESSOR ROBERTS: He certainly meant . . . Does that excuse somebody saying, "I'll lug the guts into the neighbor room"? And was he insane when he said about Rosencrantz and Guildenstern, "They are not near my conscience"? He's just murdered two people and he doesn't care?

MR. KORNSTEIN: Your Honor, all those comments strike me as perfectly appropriate as to people who were lined up against him. No, Hamlet was not paranoid. They were really after him. And if we say he was paranoid, then that becomes perhaps another element of the mental disability.

PROFESSOR ROBERTS: I'm going to suggest not that he's paranoid but that he's a very unfeeling man. I can hardly imagine anybody saying anything like (it's my favorite line in *Hamlet*), "I'll lug the guts into the neighbor room." [3.4.219]. And later on when he's hidden the body, and he says, "But indeed if you find him not within this month, you shall nose him as you go up the stairs into the lobby." [4.3.36–38].

MR. KORNSTEIN: Well, Your Honor, certainly, though, his reaction to the deaths of Rosencrantz and Guildenstern, who he viewed as being agents of his own death, is not inappropriate. I suggest that it's not a showing of a lack of sympathy, a lack of feeling, to find out that people who are going to be your potential murderers are, to use his phrase, "hoist by their own petard." It'd be perfectly normal.

JUDGE FRANKEL: Do you concede that Rosencrantz and Guildenstern are dead?

MR. KORNSTEIN: I won't be slow this time. If the court is suggesting that they're not dead, I'll accept that and get a dismissal on that ground as well.

JUDGE FRANKEL: So, whom have we got left . . . ?

MR. KORNSTEIN: Well, Claudius we know is dead. And he deserved to die much earlier. You know, Hamlet should be given an award for saving the state the money for a trial and an execution.
    Now to wrap it all up, we have a provision in our law that

allows a reversal, an acquittal in the interest of justice. It's a catch-all provision. Certainly, given the totality of the facts and the circumstances in this case, Hamlet is a prime candidate, perhaps the leading candidate in all our literary history, to have his convictions reversed and to be set out free so he can teach us some of the good things that he has been teaching us for all these many years. Thank you.

MR. GILLERS: Thank you. May it please the court, no one regrets more than the People the fact that the defendant's many, many suppression motions, and efforts at continuances, and challenges to the constitutionality of the various statutes have caused this case to last 400 years. We were ready in 1594. But finally justice has been done. However, because the case has taken 400 years to come to trial, Hamlet has been able to buy into the twentieth-century phenomenon of victimology. We hear from his counsel, today, that this man who has been convicted of killing six people, or responsible for the deaths of six people, in the course of several days, is himself a victim. He's a victim of his victims. He's a victim of political intrigue and he's a victim of society. The jury didn't buy it and neither should this panel.

I would remind the court that in Hamlet's very first soliloquy he compared his father to his uncle as, "hyperion to a satyr." Hyperion is the human embodiment of the sun god and a satyr is half man, half beast. I suggest, and we suggested below, that those were the forces fighting within Hamlet himself and ultimately he yielded to the satyr. And how do we know that? Judge Roberts, we know that from the very line you quoted. Horatio was shocked that Hamlet would seal the fate of Rosencrantz and Guildenstern by instructing in a forged document, under a forged seal, that the English king kill them, "Not shriving time allowed." No time to repent allowed. Shocked is Horatio, and what does

52

Hamlet say. "Why, man, they did make love to this employment. They are not near my conscience."

JUDGE FRANKEL: But about Rosencrantz and Guildenstern, your adversary says you may have a corpus problem.

MR. GILLERS: Oh I don't think so.

JUDGE FRANKEL: What's the evidence that they're dead?

MR. GILLERS: There was, first of all there was no challenge to it. But there was an authenticated death certificate from England brought into the court below and properly introduced in evidence.

JUDGE FRANKEL: Hasn't there been widespread evidence that they've been around this city recently?

MR. GILLERS: No, Your Honor. And I would point out that if they are alive, Hamlet has waived any objection to being convicted of their murder on that basis by failing to raise it in his brief.

JUDGE FRANKEL: Even if they're not dead, we should affirm the conviction?

MR. GILLERS: Yes, Hamlet can bring a coram nobis or a habeas corpus to challenge his conviction on that ground. But the record here is inadequate to conclude that they're not dead and Hamlet has not raised that issue in his briefs here. Now, I suggest to you that statement "They are not near my conscience" is the key to this case. It is the proof that Hamlet has become the satyr and not the hyperion that his father was.

Even with these six deaths, Hamlet may have retained

some residuum of humanity, some affection in the minds and hearts of the people of Denmark, lo, these many centuries. But now counsel adds to his several crimes the crime of remarkable chutzpah. The nerve to come here and slander the court below with an accusation of a political trial. The people proved their case meticulously, each of these six deaths.

I would like to say something about Polonius. Counsel erred, I believe, when he suggested that Hamlet slew Polonius after seeing the ghost and being in an upset state. That is not true. He slew Polonius before the ghost appeared. Polonius said, "What ho!", making it very clear that he wasn't a rat as Hamlet suggested later he might be, but a person, because the court took judicial notice that rats don't say, "What ho!" Hamlet slew Polonius believing he was the king. Earlier you recall he had refrained from slaying the king not because Hamlet was mad, but because in a very calculated way he did not want to slay the king while the king was praying. He didn't know the king was not praying, he thought he was. Now, that is the act of a very calculating man. He knew what he was doing. He thought he had the opportunity to kill the king up in the queen's bedroom. He thought it was the king. He didn't think it was an intruder in the queen's bedroom. And he killed what he thought was the king. A person who kills one person thinking it is another person is nonetheless guilty of murder.

I want to address the jurisdictional part.

JUDGE FRANKEL: Before you get to jurisdiction, and let me request you don't tell me this isn't in the briefs, I have a problem about selective prosecution in this case. We've had Othello and Macbeth and all manner of people, not to say Henry VIII and serial killing. As far as I know, none have been prosecuted. What do you say to that?

MR. GILLERS: They weren't Danish Your Honor.

JUDGE FRANKEL: I was wondering about that, and do you then say that there's a problem of ethnic discrimination here?

MR. GILLERS: If Othello had committed his crime, or Macbeth his crime, in Denmark, Your Honor, we would have prosecuted them with equal fervor.

JUDGE FRANKEL: Is that clear? Because I've copied out a line here from Ben Jonson about this great Dane whose bark was worse than his bite. Do you say that they were showing that the Danes can prosecute their own people? Is that . . .

MR. GILLERS: In Denmark, Your Honor, as Your Honor well knows, no person is above the law, not even a former prince like Hamlet, and not even a king and indeed that leads into my next point, if I may go to it Your Honor, on Claudius. Hamlet, at the time he slew Claudius, had in his pocket the letter that Claudius had written to the English king asking for Hamlet's demise. That letter would have been proof of Claudius's treachery. There was also ample evidence that would have supported a conviction of Claudius for the death of Gertrude.

JUDGE DUFFY: But wouldn't we run into the problem of sovereign immunity there?

MR. GILLERS: No, because the king in Denmark is, first of all, elected and second is below the law.

JUDGE DUFFY: Well, I suggest that just because they're elected does not mean that they don't have sovereign immunity.

MR. GILLERS: Kings may have sovereign immunity if, for example, it were a civil case where they were being charged with some kind of sexual harassment. But in a criminal case there is no sovereign immunity. Now, Hamlet having this proof of Claudius's guilt, nevertheless, knowing the sword is poisoned at this time, consciously and purposefully kills Claudius. There's no evidence of insanity at that point. The jury rejected that argument. There was a decision to kill, and a successful murder. Laertes: I think my worthy opponent has the facts slightly wrong. As Judge Roberts pointed out, there were three different ways that Claudius envisioned that Hamlet might meet his end. One was the poison in the cup, the other was the poison on the sword, and the third was the fact that the sword was unbated. That's a third and distinct way. It means that the point was exposed so that one could be wounded or killed with the point. Hamlet didn't know of any of these three ways until Laertes wounded him with the unbated sword. Hamlet then realized there was something amiss. There was an unbated sword. He got possession of that sword—he still doesn't know it has poison on it—and goes after Laertes. "Come at me," says he. The king says, "Part them. They are incensed." It is now obvious Hamlet is angry. He has lost his cool but he isn't insane. He's about to get back at Laertes for wounding him. He doesn't know the sword is poisoned. But he does know that it is unbated. He pursues Laertes and he stabs him. As it turns out, the poison operates first but that is of no moment because if there are multiple causes of a homicide and the defendant has inflicted one of those, the fact that the ultimate death is from the poison is of no moment. The defendant is still guilty of murder.

JUDGE FRANKEL: Is it clear that it was the poison?

MR. GILLERS: It was the poison.

JUDGE FRANKEL: In the record, it was the poison that killed
Laertes?

MR. GILLERS: Well, that was what Laertes said. We accept that it
was the poison.

JUDGE FRANKEL: Isn't the record also clear that Laertes was too
fat? The reason I ask you that is, suppose with that flesh
wound, Laertes had dropped dead from a coronary because
he was out of condition, would you have prosecuted here?

MR. GILLERS: We would've prosecuted but possibly for a lesser
offense. Certainly if we thought that Hamlet's intention was
to inflict a nonconsensual wound, we would have prosecuted.
Yes.

JUDGE FRANKEL: But as far as what Hamlet knew, isn't the
situation the same as if Laertes had dropped dead because of
his being overweight? He had a flesh wound that wouldn't
have killed him.

MR. GILLERS: Laertes was not overweight. He was in fine
physical condition, having been practicing fencing for years
in France. So the record shows that was . . .

JUDGE DUFFY: Are you suggesting that a fat man can't fence?

MR. GILLERS: Not at the skill and level that Laertes had attained.
Yes. I want to come to the issue of the jurisdiction for
Rosencrantz and Guildenstern. We accept that we had the
burden of proof on jurisdiction and we cited in our brief,

section 7 of Title 18 which gives this court jurisdiction of officers on the high seas, which is where Hamlet forged the death sentence for Rosencrantz and Guildenstern. So that is one basis for our jurisdiction. Another basis is that we claim the vessel was a Danish vessel. Now eminent counsel says we don't know. Maybe it was an English vessel on a return trip. But that was a decision ultimately reached on ample evidence by the court below. The record shows that on the spur of the moment in what the king called, ". . . fiery haste," it was necessary to dispatch Hamlet to England following Polonius's death. The jury could well have concluded that the only ship available to the king with such haste over which he could take command would have been a Danish vessel. That was a question for the jury, and it resolved it in our favor.

Now, that brings me to Ophelia; perhaps the most poignant and touching part of this whole story, and one where Hamlet, unfortunately for him, fares less well in 1994 then he might have in 1594. It was the theory of the people below, Your Honors, that Hamlet's strategy was essentially this: After meeting with the ghost, and I'll say more about the ghost momentarily, Hamlet was wise enough to know that you don't go killing your mother's husband, and the king of your country, because a ghost said so. He needed better evidence than that; "more relative than this," i.e., the word of a ghost. But he was also fearful that Claudius might be out for him. And so he had to protect himself, and indeed Claudius was rather suspicious as the chief judge pointed out. He was dubious that Hamlet really was as crazy as he was pretending to be. Hamlet needed time. That's what he needed most of all. And so he hit upon an idea, a brilliant idea. He would pretend to be insane; to have lost his reason. But he needed an explanation for that, for that "antic disposition." And so immediately after we hear the plan for an antic disposition, we learn that Hamlet is presenting himself as a distraught lover to Ophelia. Yes, Ophelia returned the gifts, although she didn't want to. Yes, she barred his entreaties, although she didn't want to—that made Hamlet's task even easier; to create the illusion that his mental state was a product of Ophelia's rejection. In fact, he was using her. He was using her; he was as unconcerned with her as he was with Polonius's body after he slew Polonius and as he was with Guildenstern and Rosencrantz, who he said were not near his conscience.

JUDGE FRANKEL: Why don't you come to her death, Mr. Attorney General. She fell out of a tree. Is it the position of the state that she committed suicide or that it was an accident?

MR. GILLERS: No, it's our position that it was an accident. That she indeed had lost her reason, that she did not intend to kill herself, and that she put herself in a dangerous situation.

JUDGE FRANKEL: And you think you have a case for proximate cause because a lady went crazy and fell out of a tree, that he killed her?

MR. GILLERS: Yes, we think we have a case for a negligent homicide at the least. The jury convicted of reckless homicide because of Hamlet's abandon of any concern after having encouraged Ophelia on again, off again—"Lady, shall I lie in your lap?" [3.2.110], he asked after telling her "Get thee to a nunnery!"[3.1.122] He played with her in a relentless and despicable way. She was a frail person. She didn't realize how frail she was. After seeing Hamlet in the nunnery scene, she said, "T' have seen what I have seen, see what I see!" [3.1.164]. She sees nothing. She doesn't know how to live.

Her father had to tell her and she obeyed him. Hamlet slew her father. She had no mother. Her brother was in Paris. He toyed with her. He made her mad; truly mad. And then he left her. He left her. He provided not at all. Did he ask Horatio to take care of her? No, he did not. He just disregarded her. He had a responsibility to her, having put her into that state and, today at least, if not in 1594, we can understand that at the least his failure to . . .

JUDGE DUFFY: Are you suggesting that anytime anyone writes a "Dear John" letter that they're liable for prosecution if something bad happens at the end?

MR. GILLERS: No, Your Honor, and we would not prosecute a "Dear John" letter author, and we never have in this jurisdiction. Or "Dear Jane" letter either. But we submit that this is different.

JUDGE DUFFY: Why is it different? All he did was reject her. Isn't that what a "Dear John" letter does? Reject somebody. Have you never been rejected?

MR. GILLERS: That's not in the record below Your Honor. Your Honor, this was not a rejection. If it had only been a rejection, if he had ignored her and done nothing more, we would not have added Ophelia to the indictment.

JUDGE DUFFY: You will agree that he did not intend in any way to hurt her?

MR. GILLERS: I agree. Recklessness and negligence are elements of a crime that do not require intention. If we believed he intended to do it, we might have upped the ante.

PROFESSOR ROBERTS: Is there any indication whatever that Ophelia was mad before her father died?

MR. GILLERS: She was sheltered, Your Honor.

PROFESSOR ROBERTS: She was upset, but there is no indication that I can find that she was mad before her father died, so that again, it seems to me, you might use that argument to expand your complaint against Hamlet.

MR. GILLERS: I was just coming to that. In the course of the play, Ophelia was indeed sheltered, unworldly, innocent, and thought more of herself than she actually should have. She lost the one prop in her life—after her brother had gone off to Paris, that is—her father. And then after Hamlet had had his way with her, she killed herself. She had gone mad. So, we asked the jury to find, and it did, that Hamlet was the conscious and purposeful source of her mental instability. When one person relentlessly and consciously drives another person to the mental condition that Ophelia suffered after Hamlet had finished, that first person, Hamlet, is responsible for the conduct of the victim. It is certainly objectively foreseeable. The test for negligent homicide is simply this, Judge Duffy: Whether it constitutes a gross deviation from the standard of care that a reasonable person would observe.

JUDGE DUFFY: Counselor, if you believe that people who profess love do what a reasonable person would do then I submit to you that you have missed the boat.

MR. GILLERS: No, Your Honor. That's not our point here. We would not prosecute Hamlet if he had acted as a reasonable lover, i.e., unreasonably. But we don't believe he acted as a lover. For Hamlet, our position has been that Ophelia was a tool, not an object of love.

JUDGE DUFFY: Then if you're suggesting that Ophelia was a tool then it shouldn't have been manslaughter; it should have been intentional murder.

MR. GILLERS: We don't believe he intended her death. We do recognize that there can be some cases in which "A" persuades "B" to commit suicide. We don't believe that's the situation here. And since we have five other life terms anyway . . .

JUDGE DUFFY: Well, yes, but I wonder why you're so insistent upon this one. You would think he's Dr. Kevorkian.

MR. GILLERS: Well, we think it will send a signal, Your Honor.

JUDGE DUFFY: I see.

MR. GILLERS: We think it's high time that this sort of conduct be brought to trial. We think Ophelia's rights as a human being have a claim to the attention of the court. And that's why we added her in. We don't need it. We've had him in jail for 400 years already and he'll never get out. But we think that the moral universe requires the conviction for the death of Ophelia. Now the ghost. I said I would come to the ghost. I don't think this court has to find that there was or was not a ghost. I hasten to add that Hamlet was not the only person to see the ghost. There were at least three others who saw the ghost on three successive nights, and heard the ghost cry "Swear!" (When Hamlet asked them to promise not to reveal the existence of the ghost, they did swear, so they acted on what they heard.) And most remarkably, Your Honors, the ghost knew the circumstances of King Hamlet's death. It is the kind of circumstance you don't come across every day, not even in the tabloids. Poison in the ear during sleep in the garden. That's a unique way to die. That was the way King Hamlet did in fact die, as the murder of Gonzago and the confession of Claudius ultimately establish. Now, is that a pure coincidence? Can we just write that off? I don't think so, but it doesn't matter. Because Hamlet did not do his bloody deeds based solely on the word of the ghost. He had proof "more relative than" that. Brilliantly! Brilliantly, he staged the play within the play and obtained his demeanor evidence of Claudius's guilt. Demeanor evidence is also admissible in court. If Hamlet had had the good sense to withdraw from the fray with Laertes, as soon as he realized that the sword was unbated, which he could have done because he was not in mortal danger then, he already had ample proof to convict Claudius of murdering Gertrude and also of a plot on his own life and perhaps show the guilt of Polonius as well. That would have been the way to do it. That would have been the way that a real mensch would have behaved, which Hamlet by this time, a real satyr, was not. And so I suggest to this court, in conclusion, that here we have a man who has wiped out a family of three, and caused the death of three others. All in a matter of days. Who has the arrogance now to come before this court and say his murder convictions ought to be dismissed in the interests of justice. What about justice for the victims? The six decedents, their friends, society. Never has this court reversed a homicide conviction in the interest of justice. Justice commands that Hamlet stay exactly where he is forever more. Thank you.

MR. KORNSTEIN: A brief rebuttal, Your Honors. My reaction to the attorney general's presentation really is three words. "Let's get real!" The only signal that would be sent by convicting Hamlet for Ophelia's death is never break up with someone you're dating. I'm not sure that that's a good message to be sent. Everyone else except Polonius, who ended up dead, was in league against Hamlet. They were all trying to kill Hamlet. I mean, that's the reality of what's happening here. It's not as if these six dead bodies were entirely innocent bystanders and Hamlet drove some chariot into the middle of a crowd. They were all conspiring to get him. Maybe he didn't do everything that he might have done. Maybe he was a little overwrought. But to come into court and to have the representative of the government discuss ghosts as some sort of legitimating reason to get some defendant a life sentence, trivializes the court and embarrasses the concept of justice. Are we back in the time of the Salem witch trials? What else are we going to talk about? Are we going backward full speed?

Now the attorney general talked about elevated notions in the 1990s that would increase the ambit of liability. The fact is that heart balm statutes that imposed civil liability for breaking a promise to marry were abolished long ago. So not only is there no civil liability, a fortiori there should be no criminal liability in the Ophelia situation.

Now Polonius is the toughest argument for Hamlet's counsel to make. That we frankly recognize. But we have to focus that situation. What was Polonius doing in Gertrude's bedroom? And how was Hamlet to know that it was Polonius? Should he have talked? Should he have asked for an ID card? What should he have done in—

JUDGE DUFFY: Counselor, if you had been in the queen's bedroom—

MR. KORNSTEIN: Not me, Your Honor!

JUDGE DUFFY: I see. He didn't care, is what you're suggesting, whom he killed.

MR. KORNSTEIN: I would phrase it slightly differently. He was going to kill whomever was behind that curtain. Whomever it was.

JUDGE DUFFY: Intentionally.

MR. KORNSTEIN: He intended to put his sword through whomever was behind that curtain.

JUDGE DUFFY: So isn't that intentional murder?

MR. KORNSTEIN: We think it fits the defense of justification that given all the evil doings going on, he was defending the queen's bedroom. He didn't know what was going to happen. There had been a murder there recently.

JUDGE FRANKEL: Do you say this was a political killing?

MR. KORNSTEIN: The killing of Polonius?

JUDGE FRANKEL: Yes.

MR. KORNSTEIN: I'm not sure I understand the phrase "political killing."

JUDGE FRANKEL: Well I thought you had said at some point it's a political trial.

MR. KORNSTEIN: It is a political trial.

JUDGE FRANKEL: Well I remember Polonius and that business of no borrowing and no lending, which seems to me would have obstructed the whole development toward capitalism.

MR. KORNSTEIN: He might have added, "And don't go in the queen's bedroom."

JUDGE FRANKEL: Well, and if Hamlet hadn't done him in, Denmark might still be a feudal state. Does that give justification? I don't know what you meant by political killings.

MR. KORNSTEIN: I said it was a political trial, not political killing. I think that because of this foreign despot on the Danish throne—Fortinbras has no claim, he just took over—that the purpose that Hamlet was tried, and the reason that he's still in prison is because Fortinbras, unlike other enlightened despots, when we show some force, did not resign and move to another country. For those reasons we ask for a reversal. Thank you.

PROFESSOR ROBERTS: My understanding is that we are now going to have some deliberation on the part of the judges, and we will do it in order, briefly, starting with Judge Frankel, and then I hope we will give you some chance to make your comments and conclusions as well.

JUDGE FRANKEL: Well, my notes, and I'll try to be brief, which is not my habit, are under the headings of each of the alleged victims. I would acquit on the charge of killing Ophelia. I feel Ophelia who, incidentally, was a disgrace to the whole feminist movement, brought it on herself. At worst, I think, she reflects what one of the gravediggers I think was talking about. She apparently committed suicide in self-defense and

I don't think that that's a kind of death for which Hamlet should be held liable. She was acting in self-defense, and Hamlet helped her. I think that's virtuous, rather than vicious. So, when we come to vote, I think I'd find him not guilty on the count respecting Ophelia.

JUDGE DUFFY: I would have to agree with my brother here. Ophelia didn't . . . I can't see how Ophelia gets to be a victim of Hamlet in this particular thing, other than perhaps because she was portraying what she thought a feminist of that age should do. But I don't see any criminal responsibility whatsoever for Hamlet.

PROFESSOR ROBERTS: Is that it?

JUDGE DUFFY: Yeah, not guilty. You want me go through the rest? I've got some—

PROFESSOR ROBERTS: Yeah, why don't you? Well, should we talk about Ophelia? Let's all talk about Ophelia. I agree with the gentlemen on Ophelia. I don't think she committed suicide. I think that she had been warned right from the start that Hamlet could not, would not, marry her and I don't think she was driven mad by him. Although, I understood that the attorney general said that Hamlet had had his way with her. Maybe that would drive you mad. I don't see any evidence that happened however. So I would agree with you on Ophelia. I don't think there're any grounds at all for accusing Hamlet of murder, or manslaughter.

JUDGE FRANKEL: My next notes, which are also brief, are about Rosencrantz and Guildenstern. And my position, very simply, is, I don't think the record establishes at all that they are really dead. This thing says "use the mike please," which leads me to ask what the hell was everybody laughing about? Somebody back there is telling jokes obviously. In any event, I do not accept that Rosencrantz and Guildenstern are dead. There is plenty of evidence of which I think the record contains some and if not, we can take judicial notice that they have indeed been heard of around these parts, in very recent years, not 400 years ago. And even as to the recent reappearance, I don't believe Tom Stoppard. I don't know that they died even recently. So I think as I raised with the attorney general, that he's got an insurmountable problem of having no corpus at all and certainly no corpus delicti and I would acquit for Rosencrantz and Guildenstern on that ground.

JUDGE DUFFY: I would convict. I would believe that not only do we have a corpus, but a dead corpus, or corpi. It's clear that Hamlet did his damndest to have the two of them knocked off and felt that they justly deserved it. But in so doing, Hamlet set himself up as a court, judge, jury, and executioner. The only thing he did was to use the tool of the English crown and as you know, as an Irishman, you know what I think of the English crown as a tool. But all he did was use the crown to do his dirty work. I would convict.

PROFESSOR ROBERTS: First of all, we do have the evidence of the ambassador from England who says, "We did it. Rosencrantz and Guildenstern are dead. When do we get paid off?" So I believe they are dead, and I hold Hamlet morally, if not legally responsible for their deaths. I think it's the most callous thing that he did because it was premeditated and without reason. You don't kill somebody because you suspect them of conspiring against you. And there is not even any evidence that they did conspire against him. I wonder, and I think, and I'm now touching on one of the secrets of the success of this play: I think the audience really wants Hamlet to kill Claudius. But I think the audience in Elizabethan England believed the Old Testament "Thou shalt not kill." and "vengeance is mine and I will repay sayeth the Lord." So I think that's the worst thing Hamlet did.

JUDGE DUFFY: They were basically fools who were being used. That's the way I view it.

PROFESSOR ROBERTS: And we feel some affinity with—

JUDGE DUFFY: A fool who has been used. Yes!

JUDGE FRANKEL: Well I think some wise person said that a dissent speaks to the better wisdom of the future ages. So I think when Hamlet comes on for retrial in a few hundred years, his innocence, with respect to Rosencrantz and Guildenstern, will be more apparent than it is to my distinguished colleagues. My next note concerns Laertes. I consider that Laertes is the guiltiest of all the people involved in this tragic situation. Seems clear to me that Laertes orchestrated this whole story of carnage from beginning to end and that he did this wantonly and viciously in the hope that he could cover up for all time, which he has failed to do, his long history of incestuous relationships with his sister. So my position is perfectly clear: if it were possible to revive the dead, unlike the situation with the living, I would think Laertes is the one who should have been on trial in this case and should have been convicted of all these killings. It follows perfectly clearly that I would acquit Hamlet for his well-deserved death.

JUDGE DUFFY: Laertes gives me some problems, too, but for other reasons. I'm not willing to accuse him of incest but of actively plotting the death of Hamlet. That is clear that he did. And just because what happened, happened basically through mistake, can we say there is evidence sufficient to hold Hamlet guilty of intentional murder? That is, intending the death of this person, if he merely gave him a wound such as was suggested German students were wont to do, I don't see that he intended to kill him. And since there's no proof that he intended to kill him, I would have to say that as far as Laertes is concerned, the conviction would have to be overturned.

PROFESSOR ROBERTS: I think I agree with that because I think that Hamlet was angry at being wounded by a sword that was supposed to have a bate on it. And he was justifiably angry, I think. He did not, I agree, mean to kill Laertes, and, in fact, even if he had, he was in the heat of battle. I think Laertes is quite right when he says, "He is justly killed with his own trap." And so I would, I would . . . what's the proper terminology? I would . . .

JUDGE DUFFY: Affirm his conviction.

PROFESSOR ROBERTS: Affirm . . . No!

JUDGE DUFFY: This is what is known as influencing the Chief Judge.

PROFESSOR ROBERTS: I would overturn his conviction for Laertes, Hamlet's conviction.

JUDGE DUFFY: Okay.

JUDGE FRANKEL: Well, I, having voted to upset the convictions with respect to the four others, a little bit reluctantly, I find myself voting to affirm with respect to Claudius and Polonius.

Very simply, I take the view, I think with entire detachment, that old gentlemen like them, however vicious or boring, should be treated gently, and should hardly ever be murdered. Taking that view, although I would only affirm with respect to two of the six alleged victims, I confront, for myself at least, a question that's always interested me. The question of sentencing. And I conclude that rather remarkable longevity does not justify a sentence of approximately 400 years. So I would sentence Hamlet to time served and free him on that score.

JUDGE DUFFY: I have a feeling that the question of sentence came up because a suggestion was made by someone that I hold the Eastern Intercollegiate records in sentencing. But, let's talk about whether he should be convicted. Poor Polonius . . . was just that, poor Polonius. And Hamlet didn't care who he was killing. As far as I'm concerned, that's murder. And there was no justification whatsoever. The claim that he was crazy, is crazy like a fox, particularly when it's put together with a claim that he's entitled to be the sovereign of the country. As far as the sentence is concerned, ah, you know, it's just a lifetime or two.

PROFESSOR ROBERTS: One thing that gave me great pleasure was the final proof that Dr. Samuel Johnson is still alive, that we can quote him. . . . I think Polonius is a clear case of murder. I think Hamlet clearly knew . . . he thought he was killing Claudius. Would that be better? He says, "I took thee for thy better." There's only one person around who fit that category. And I think, as you pointed out, he knew he was killing somebody. He didn't kill the person he meant to kill, but it was still murder. Shall I deal also with Claudius? I have to say that the biggest mistake is that Hamlet is a hero, but he is only a hero if he dies in the end. And bringing him back to life was a bad mistake. I think that an Elizabethan audience would have wanted him to kill Claudius, but they would have only let him get by with that if he were dead at the end. I agree with the attorney general that Hamlet could have made a case against Claudius, but I think that in the heat of that moment when he saw his mother die, that it's maybe understandable homicide. That is, I'm not sure that that's not something that we can get him off the hook for. So I have a lot of trouble with Claudius. Ideally he shouldn't have killed Claudius. Emotionally, he had to, and that leaves me uncertain but since I'm so certain about Polonius and Rosencrantz and Guildenstern, it doesn't matter.

JUDGE DUFFY: I think it's up to them.

PROFESSOR ROBERTS: I think it's up to you.

JUDGE DUFFY: On Claudius? Look, Claudius as far as the playwright was concerned really deserved it. He was the one guy in the entire thing who deserved to get knocked off. Was it murder? Sure it was. And I would affirm as to Claudius. He deserved to die, but that doesn't mean that even a prince could set himself up to be the person to hear all the evidence; to do all the investigation; hear all the evidence; to decide the fate of the man and to execute him. No. That is something even a reigning sovereign should not be permitted to do, and I think that's murder, too.

NORMAN GREENE: It's not too ordinary in an appeal to ask for questions and answers, but we're going to try here. This is an experimental situation. So, anyone who wants to ask a question, go right up to the mike, and I'll call on you. The questions can be to any of the judges or to Dan Kornstein or Stephen Gillers. Yes, go ahead.

FIRST QUESTIONER: Attorney here in New York. Just curious, for the attorneys, what effect, and maybe this is looking to a possible appeal from this judgment, what effect they think the fact that Denmark is now part of the European Union, and is subject to the rules of various strictures of that union including things like human rights, special commission for that purpose, and how that might affect an appeal?

NORMAN GREENE: Who is that directed to?

FIRST QUESTIONER: Either attorney who might want to take it up.

NORMAN GREENE: You want to try Dan?

MR. KORNSTEIN: Well, we already have our petition to appeal prepared and if that should fail, we will be asking for a pardon, and if that should fail we'd be asking for general amnesty.

NORMAN GREENE: Yes, what's your name please?

SECOND QUESTIONER: I'm a layman. My comment is addressed to, forgive me, Your Honor, I didn't catch your name.

JUDGE DUFFY: Oh, my name is Duffy . . . just . . .

SECOND QUESTIONER: Duffy . . . Well, it seems to me that you showed some prejudice when you remarked regarding Rosencrantz and Guildenstern, when you remarked, when you gave your opinion regarding the British Crown. I'm just wondering whether this had any effect on the decision?

JUDGE DUFFY: It's true, I have a prejudice toward the British Crown, or against the British Crown, but I assure you it had no impact whatsoever.

THIRD QUESTIONER: I'm also an attorney in New York.

JUDGE DUFFY: Get closer young man.

THIRD QUESTIONER: The question I have I guess is directed at
Judge Duffy. You sort of, I think, hit the nail on the head
when you said a prince has no right. The issue, I think, in
this play is: Is Hamlet acting as a prince or is Hamlet acting
as the person who should have been the rightful king of
Denmark. As the rightful king of Denmark, he would have
been entitled to mete out justice as he would see fit, as kings
in that time would have been expected to.

JUDGE DUFFY: But don't you agree that the people of Denmark
did not recognize Hamlet as their actual king. If they had, the
play would have been substantially different.

THIRD QUESTIONER: Well . . .

JUDGE DUFFY: Instead, Claudius is their king and so recognized
by all of the people.

THIRD QUESTIONER: There is commentary and discussion that
Claudius's ascension to the throne was fairly rapid and
accomplished at a time when the king's son and heir was out
of the country.

JUDGE DUFFY: Oh listen, I'm not suggesting that a claim could not
have been made that Claudius improperly took the crown.
But that still doesn't give a prince, a person who has not been
accepted as king, the rights of sovereignty.

THIRD QUESTIONER: Well, I suppose it may not give him the
rights of sovereignty as might have been conferred by the

people, but if the play is about whether, if the play is about the difference, perhaps, between kings and men and how men might have to act, and how kings have to act, and how that is different, then I think what you have is a situation where Hamlet, believing himself to be the rightful king takes it upon himself to cure the ills that beset the rotten Denmark.

JUDGE DUFFY: Counselor, I suggest to you that I have run into some defendants, who, believe or not, think that they are the rightful kings. They are not too happy with me, I will admit that. But no, you can't go that far. The people did not accept him. And more than that, think of what the whole doctrine of sovereign immunity evolved from. Sovereign immunity evolves from the fact that the judges knew which side their bread was buttered on. If they held the king, who had the power to lop off their heads, to have done something wrong, then they would be headless judges. Now, headless judges unlike the Headless Horseman do not appear on Halloween, and we will have no such suggestion about that. No, there's no way that Hamlet can get off with that kind of a claim as far as I'm concerned.

NORMAN GREENE: I would like to take a couple of more questions, and then what we're going to do is let the advocates respond to the judges. Yes?

FOURTH QUESTIONER: I'd like the chief judge to comment on an observation I've made. We're faced, in Claudius, with an interesting character, character who is certainly flawed, having committed one, perhaps two unpardonable acts, but who then turns into a magnificent ruler. For example, faced with an imminent invasion he prepares night and day to defend, we're given to understand, a defenseless kingdom.

And then, nonetheless, by exercising magnificent diplomacy turns the invading force against another traditional enemy, offering nothing but a march across his territory. Who would have been a better king? And were not the electors very wise in following, probably, the counsel of Polonius, in electing Claudius rather than Hamlet as the king?

PROFESSOR ROBERTS: I think you make an excellent point. I think at the beginning particularly, you have a sense that Claudius is a gracious, protective man, that he loves his wife, and I think you have the sense at least superficially, that he's a good king. There is some indication that maybe he drinks a lot.

FOURTH QUESTIONER: May I comment on that?

JUDGE DUFFY: Nothing wrong with that . . .

PROFESSOR ROBERTS: I'm with you.

FOURTH QUESTIONER: Winston Churchill did it. A number of years ago, I saw a performance in London that struck me for only one point. The drunkenness is not Claudius, but Gertrude. And if you go through the text again you find some absolutely phenomenal points that are made if you portray Gertrude as a lush. What does Hamlet mean by, "To the manner born?"

PROFESSOR ROBERTS: By what?

FOURTH QUESTIONER: "To the manner born." "Though I am native here and to the manner born." [1.4.14–15]. Speaking of drunkenness, he wasn't born to Claudius, he was born to Gertrude. The scene in which Gertrude describes the death of Ophelia is made particularly poignant by having her portrayed as carrying a goblet and drinking while she's describing that. Excuse me. And at the end, the death of Gertrude played as Gertrude standing on one side of the stage and Claudius at the other, Gertrude lifts this goblet as if to drink, and Claudius says, "Gertrude, do not drink." And she says, "I will, my lord, I pray you pardon me." [5.2.293–94]. As if that conversation, "Don't drink!" "I will!" has happened a million times before. It works in performance.

NORMAN GREENE: Can we take the next question over here? This fellow has been waiting . . .

PROFESSOR ROBERTS: Let me say one more thing about that. Gertrude needs all the help she can get on the stage because she's not there. She's not a character. And if you can make her drunk, at least you see something. I would, just in answer to your question, I think that Claudius might, in many ways, have been a better ruler but he still would have been a murderer and I prefer not to be ruled by a murderer.

NORMAN GREENE: Two more questions before we have the advocates.

FIFTH QUESTIONER: I would ask Judge Duffy, wasn't the English king in 1776 the recognized king?

JUDGE DUFFY: Sure he was. Did he have the consent of the governed? It's a different thing with Claudius. Obviously he did have the consent of the governed because there was nobody who took up arms, save Hamlet. Nobody was willing to knock him off. It's a little tough to say it's the same type of thing.

FIFTH QUESTIONER: Isn't the issue in a criminal prosecution such as this as to whether there was colorable authority to do what he did?

JUDGE DUFFY: Colorable authority to commit regicide? That he believed that he was acting as a representative of the state. Well that's almost, again, getting back to the diminished mental capacity, you know, I can't see it.

SIXTH QUESTIONER: I have an ethical question, more in the philosophical sense than in the legal sense. We're talking here about a system of laws that supposes that everyone including even the head of state and even the head of government is subject to the laws. The attorney general here suggested that Hamlet's correct course of action after obtaining evidence of Claudius's guilt was to marshal that evidence and take it over to the attorney general and have Claudius prosecuted? As an ethical matter, as a matter of moral philosophy, what is one to do when one has an unjust tyrannical ruler who is not subject to law, who is not subject, who cannot be held to account in any legal way?

MR. GILLERS: Well, you can try to overthrow him and, if you're right, I guess you escape punishment, if you win, and if you don't, you're guilty. I mean it's a matter of pure power isn't it?

SIXTH QUESTIONER: I mean, is revolution in that sense any worse than, any better than regicide?

MR. GILLERS: Listen, if it's not in the Code of Professional Responsibility. . . . I don't know.

NORMAN GREENE: If we can make it very quick with the next few questions, we'll finish it up because I want to give the advocates a chance.

JUDGE DUFFY: I'm going to give up my time to questions from the audience. I'll talk to them.

SEVENTH QUESTIONER: I'm an actor and a Shakespearean student. My question concerns reasonable doubt on Polonius. I grant that there are arguments both ways. That Hamlet might have known that it was Polonius, but I strongly suggest that, and I ask you to put yourself mentally in this situation, you're in someone's room, and you hear a noise from some hidden area. Excuse me, who are you please, where is your calling card? I mean, you take the situation as it's presented. I'll refer you to Shakespeare *Henry V,* "I took you for the knight, for the costume you pretend to be." A noise comes from behind the curtain. I mean, you have to react based on that situation, and at the very least, you have to resolve the doubt in favor of Hamlet as far as whether he killed Polonius, whether he murdered Polonius.

MR. KORNSTEIN: I agree.

NORMAN GREENE: Would you like to . . . do you have a question for Judge Duffy on his prejudice toward the English Crown?

EIGHTH QUESTIONER: No, I can talk to him about that later. I have a question about how each of you said that Hamlet was not responsible for Ophelia's death. And I think that's an error. From what I remember the phrase "Get thee to a nunnery" was a slang term for a whorehouse, not a convent, as most people think of it. And so when he was doing that he was really impugning her good reputation and the honor of the time that she was an emotionally battered woman that she had to take her own life to preserve her honor. And I think that's reversible error, on your part, and I'd like you to comment. Thank you.

79

JUDGE DUFFY: I've got to ask you a question and I, by the way, may agree with the result that is suggested by the question: would you suggest that most of these rap stars with their rap songs, which are absolutely offensive, should be all taken and chucked in the prison along with Hamlet, because they have written these violent things? I was riding up in the car tonight and I was not in charge of the radio, and there was something, as far as I was concerned, was absolutely vile. I doubt if any of you folks have listened to this stuff, but if you have, maybe you would think that maybe that's a good way to get rid of the rap stars of today. But I don't think that just saying things is enough to convict somebody of murder.

NORMAN GREENE: Next question?

PROFESSOR ROBERTS: Let me say something about that. That nunnery line is one of the terrible things that some critic inflicted on the world. I think that it's clear from that scene when he says, "Get thee to a nunnery!" he means get thee to a nunnery, and not to a whorehouse. He has been expressing his revulsion against women, and he's certainly not telling her to go to a whorehouse. It is true that nunnery sometimes meant whorehouse, but I don't think it means that in that scene.

JUDGE DUFFY: Nor is it a suggestion that she kill herself. He was saying "Go find a use for your life, in a nunnery."

PROFESSOR ROBERTS: One more time, I don't think she killed herself. He may have disabled her but he didn't kill her.

NORMAN GREENE: I wanted to ask you since Hamlet didn't have the original idea of the ghost, the ghost idea was certainly suggested to him by at least Horatio and some other people, and they saw the ghost first, do you think he was joining their group, or their cult or their suggestion, when he was following their idea of a ghost instructing him to do such things?

PROFESSOR ROBERTS: I don't know . . . who wants to talk about the ghost? Would you like to speak on the ghost?

MR. GILLERS: Within the four corners of the play, I think the ghost is real. I believe there was a ghost. I mean, the ghost knew too much. A ghost who knows that much must be a real ghost.

JUDGE DUFFY: Or is a ghost just a manner and means for the playwright to get across the truth of the accusations being made?

NINTH QUESTIONER: This is to Mr. Kornstein. I assume that your client would be completely satisfied with the defense of his case, but I wanted you to comment on a portion of the play, and I'm sure you know the text far better than I, in the graveyard scene. There's a presumption I believe on the part of your client that one of the skulls belongs to that of a lawyer . . .

MR. KORNSTEIN: What he says, before he picks up Yorick's skull, he picks up the first skull and says "Why may not this be the skull of a lawyer?" And then he goes on for about fifteen or twenty lines talking about where his "tenures" and "cases" are, and he could have done this and that, and then he has a line in it, "Where be his quiddities and quillities his tricks and his cases now?" I think it's an interesting jumping-off point to meditate on what is a skull of a lawyer, and not from the outside, but the inside. What does it mean to think like a lawyer, to act like a lawyer. What are the habits of thought of a lawyer, and it becomes a nice little meditation.

MR. GILLERS: I think that speech reveals a certain self-satisfaction in Hamlet in finding a dead lawyer. As a law student, that's right, he's a law student at Wittenberg.

JUDGE DUFFY: Do you think Shakespeare got charged too much?

NORMAN GREENE: Are there any other questions? Dan, you want to take the first shot at the panel?

MR. KORNSTEIN: No, I pass.

NORMAN GREENE: Steve?

MR. GILLERS: I do think that if not in 1994, maybe 400 years from today we'll be able to give Ophelia her day in court. I think she is a victim of calculated emotional abuse, and the question will be whether Hamlet's treatment of her was reasonable under contemporary community standards or a gross deviation of appropriate behavior. Apparently it may not be unreasonable even today, but stick around Ophelia, your day will come.

NORMAN GREENE: Seeing no more questions, we want to thank the panel, the judges, the advocates, and thank you all for coming.

HAMLET, PRINCE OF DENMARK

Dramatis Personae

GHOST of *Hamlet, the former King of Denmark*
CLAUDIUS, *King of Denmark, the former King's brother*
GERTRUDE, *Queen of Denmark, widow of the former King and now wife of*
    Claudius
HAMLET, *Prince of Denmark, son of the late King and of Gertrude*

POLONIUS, *councillor to the King*
LAERTES, *his son*
OPHELIA, *his daughter*
REYNALDO, *his servant*

HORATIO, *Hamlet's friend and fellow student*

VOLTIMAND,
CORNELIUS,
ROSENCRANTZ,
GUILDENSTERN,   } *members of the Danish court*
OSRIC,
A GENTLEMAN,
A LORD,

BERNARDO,
FRANCISCO,   } *officers and soldiers on watch*
MARCELLUS,

FORTINBRAS, *Prince of Norway*
CAPTAIN *in his army*

Three or Four PLAYERS, *taking the roles of* PROLOGUE, PLAYER KING, PLAYER
    QUEEN, *and* LUCIANUS
Two MESSENGERS
FIRST SAILOR
Two CLOWNS, *a gravedigger and his companion*
PRIEST
FIRST AMBASSADOR *from England*

Lords, Soldiers, Attendants, Guards, other Players, Followers of Laertes, other
    Sailors, another Ambassador or Ambassadors from England

84

ACT I

Scene I. Elsinore Castle, Denmark.

Enter Bernardo and Francisco, two sentinels, [meeting].

BERNARDO: Who's there?
FRANCISCO: Nay, answer me. Stand and unfold yourself.
BERNARDO: Long live the King!
FRANCISCO: Bernardo?
BERNARDO: He. 5
FRANCISCO: You come most carefully upon your hour.
BERNARDO: 'Tis now struck twelve. Get thee to bed, Francisco.
FRANCISCO: For this relief much thanks. 'Tis bitter cold,
    And I am sick at heart.
BERNARDO: Have you had quiet guard? 10
FRANCISCO: Not a mouse stirring.
BERNARDO: Well, good night.
    If you do meet Horatio and Marcellus,
    The rivals of my watch, bid them make haste.

Enter Horatio and Marcellus.

FRANCISCO: I think I hear them.—Stand, ho! Who is there? 15
HORATIO: Friends to this ground.
MARCELLUS: And liegemen to the Dane.
FRANCISCO: Give you good night.
MARCELLUS: O, farewell, honest soldier. Who hath relieved you?
FRANCISCO: Bernardo hath my place. Give you good night. 20

                             Exit Francisco.

MARCELLUS: Holla! Bernardo!
BERNARDO: Say, what, is Horatio there?
HORATIO: A piece of him.
BERNARDO: Welcome, Horatio. Welcome, good Marcellus.
HORATIO: What, has this thing appeared again tonight? 25
BERNARDO: I have seen nothing.
MARCELLUS: Horatio says 'tis but our fantasy,
    And will not let belief take hold of him
    Touching this dreaded sight twice seen of us.
    Therefore I have entreated him along 30
    With us to watch the minutes of this night,
    That if again this apparition come
    He may approve our eyes and speak to it.
HORATIO: Tush, tush, 'twill not appear.
BERNARDO: Sit down awhile, 35
    And let us once again assail your ears,

That are so fortified against our story,
What we have two nights seen.
HORATIO: Well, sit we down,
And let us hear Bernardo speak of this.
BERNARDO: Last night of all,
When yond same star that's westward from the pole   40
Had made his course t' illume that part of heaven
Where now it burns, Marcellus and myself,
The bell then beating one—

Enter Ghost.

MARCELLUS: Peace, break thee off! Look where it comes again!
BERNARDO: In the same figure like the King that's dead.   45
MARCELLUS: Thou art a scholar. Speak to it, Horatio.
BERNARDO: Looks 'a not like the King? Mark it, Horatio.
HORATIO: Most like. It harrows me with fear and wonder.
BERNARDO: It would be spoke to.
MARCELLUS: Speak to it, Horatio.
HORATIO: What art thou that usurp'st this time of night,   50
Together with that fair and warlike form
In which the majesty of buried Denmark
Did sometime march? By heaven, I charge thee speak!
MARCELLUS: It is offended.
BERNARDO: See, it stalks away.   55
HORATIO: Stay! Speak, speak! I charge thee, speak!

Exit Ghost.

MARCELLUS: 'Tis gone and will not answer.
BERNARDO: How now, Horatio? You tremble and look pale.
Is not this something more than fantasy?
What think you on 't?
HORATIO: Before my God, I might not this believe   60
Without the sensible and true avouch
Of mine own eyes.
MARCELLUS: Is it not like the King?
HORATIO: As thou art to thyself.
Such was the very armor he had on
When he the ambitious Norway combated.   65
So frowned he once when, in an angry parle,
He smote the sledded Polacks on the ice.
'Tis strange.
MARCELLUS: Thus twice before, and jump at this dead hour,
With martial stalk hath he gone by our watch.   70
HORATIO: In what particular thought to work I know not,
But in the gross and scope of mine opinion
This bodes some strange eruption to our state.

MARCELLUS: Good now, sit down, and tell me, he that knows,
Why this same strict and most observant watch   75
So nightly toils the subject of the land,
And why such daily cast of brazen cannon
And foreign mart for implements of war,
Why such impress of shipwrights, whose sore task
Does not divide the Sunday from the week.   80
What might be toward, that this sweaty haste
Doth make the night joint-laborer with the day?
Who is 't that can inform me?
HORATIO: That can I;
At least, the whisper goes so. Our last king,
Whose image even but now appeared to us,   85
Was, as you know, by Fortinbras of Norway,
Thereto pricked on by a most emulate pride,
Dared to the combat; in which our valiant Hamlet—
For so this side of our known world esteemed him—
Did slay this Fortinbras; who by a sealed compact   90
Well ratified by law and heraldry
Did forfeit, with his life, all those his lands
Which he stood seized of to the conqueror;
Against the which a moiety competent
Was gagèd by our king, which had returned   95
To the inheritance of Fortinbras
Had he been vanquisher, as, by the same covenant
And carriage of the article designed,
His fell to Hamlet. Now, sir, young Fortinbras,
Of unimprovèd mettle hot and full,   100
Hath in the skirts of Norway here and there
Sharked up a list of lawless resolutes
For food and diet to some enterprise
That hath a stomach in 't, which is no other—
As it doth well appear unto our state—   105
But to recover of us, by strong hand
And terms compulsatory, those foresaid lands
So by his father lost. And this, I take it,
Is the main motive of our preparations,
The source of this our watch, and the chief head   110
Of this posthaste and rummage in the land.
BERNARDO: I think it be no other but e'en so.
Well may it sort that this portentous figure
Comes armèd through our watch so like the King
That was and is the question of these wars.   115
HORATIO: A mote it is to trouble the mind's eye.
In the most high and palmy state of Rome,
A little ere the mightiest Julius fell,
The graves stood tenantless and the sheeted dead
Did squeak and gibber in the Roman streets;   120

As stars with trains of fire and dews of blood,
Disasters in the sun; and the moist star
Upon whose influence Neptune's empire stands
Was sick almost to doomsday with eclipse.
And even the like precurse of feared events, 125
As harbingers preceding still the fates
And prologue to the omen coming on,
Have heaven and earth together demonstrated
Unto our climatures and countrymen.

Enter Ghost.

But soft, behold! Lo, where it comes again! 130
I'll cross it, though it blast me. (*It spreads his arms.*)
   Stay, illusion!
If thou hast any sound or use of voice,
Speak to me!
If there be any good thing to be done
That may to thee do ease and grace to me, 135
Speak to me!
If thou art privy to thy country's fate,
Which, happily, foreknowing may avoid,
O, speak!
Or if thou hast uphoarded in thy life 140
Extorted treasure in the womb of earth,
For which, they say, you spirits oft walk in death,
Speak of it! (*The cock crows.*) Stay and speak!—
   Stop it, Marcellus.
MARCELLUS: Shall I strike at it with my partisan?
HORATIO: Do, if it will not stand. 145

[They strike at it.]

BERNARDO: 'Tis here!
HORATIO: 'Tis here!

Exit Ghost.

MARCELLUS: 'Tis gone.
We do it wrong, being so majestical,
To offer it the show of violence, 150
For it is as the air invulnerable,
And our vain blows malicious mockery.
BERNARDO: It was about to speak when the cock crew.
HORATIO: And then it started like a guilty thing
Upon a fearful summons. I have heard 155
The cock, that is the trumpet to the morn,
Doth with his lofty and shrill-sounding throat

Awake the god of day, and at his warning,
Whether in sea or fire, in earth or air,
Th' extravagant and erring spirit hies   160
To his confine; and of the truth herein
This present object made probation.
MARCELLUS: It faded on the crowing of the cock.
    Some say that ever 'gainst that season comes
    Wherein our Savior's birth is celebrated,   165
    This bird of dawning singeth all night long,
    And then, they say, no spirit dare stir abroad;
    The nights are wholesome, then no planets strike,
    No fairy takes, nor witch hath power to charm,
    So hallowed and so gracious is that time.   170
HORATIO: So have I heard and do in part believe it.
    But, look, the morn in russet mantle clad
    Walks o'er the dew of yon high eastward hill.
    Break we our watch up, and by my advice
    Let us impart what we have seen tonight   175
    Unto young Hamlet; for upon my life,
    This spirit, dumb to us, will speak to him.
    Do you consent we shall acquaint him with it,
    As needful in our loves, fitting our duty?
MARCELLUS: Let's do 't, I pray, and I this morning know   180
    Where we shall find him most conveniently.

                                                    Exeunt.

ACT I. SCENE II

*Flourish. Enter Claudius, King of Denmark, Gertrude the Queen, [the] Council,
as Polonius and his son Laertes, Hamlet, cum aliis [including Voltimand and
Cornelius].*

KING: Though yet of Hamlet our dear brother's death
    The memory be green, and that it us befitted
    To bear our hearts in grief and our whole kingdom
    To be contracted in one brow of woe,
    Yet so far hath discretion fought with nature   5
    That we with wisest sorrow think on him
    Together with remembrance of ourselves.
    Therefore our sometime sister, now our queen,
    Th' imperial jointress to this warlike state,
    Have we, as 'twere with a defeated joy—   10
    With an auspicious and a dropping eye,
    With mirth in funeral and with dirge in marriage,
    In equal scale weighing delight and dole—
    Taken to wife. Nor have we herein barred
    Your better wisdoms, which have freely gone   15

With this affair along. For all, our thanks.
Now follows that you know young Fortinbras,
Holding a weak supposal of our worth,
Or thinking by our late dear brother's death
Our state to be disjoint and out of frame,   20
Colleaguèd with this dream of his advantage,
He hath not failed to pester us with message
Importing the surrender of those lands
Lost by his father, with all bonds of law,
To our most valiant brother. So much for him.   25
Now for ourself and for this time of meeting.
Thus much the business is: we have here writ
To Norway, uncle of young Fortinbras—
Who, impotent and bedrid, scarcely hears
Of this his nephew's purpose—to suppress   30
His further gait herein, in that the levies,
The lists, and full proportions are all made
Out of his subject; and we here dispatch
You, good Cornelius, and you, Voltimand,
For bearers of this greeting to old Norway,   35
Giving to you no further personal power
To business with the King more than the scope
Of these dilated articles allow.

[He gives a paper.]

Farewell, and let your haste commend your duty.
CORNELIUS, VOLTIMAND: In that, and all things, will we show our duty.   40
KING: We doubt it nothing. Heartily farewell.

Exeunt Voltimand and Cornelius.

And now, Laertes, what's the news with you?
You told us of some suit; what is 't, Laertes?
You cannot speak of reason to the Dane
And lose your voice. What wouldst thou beg, Laertes,   45
That shall not be my offer, not thy asking?
The head is not more native to the heart,
The hand more instrumental to the mouth,
Than is the throne of Denmark to thy father.
What wouldst thou have, Laertes?   50
LAERTES: My dread lord,
    Your leave and favor to return to France,
    From whence though willingly I came to Denmark
    To show my duty in your coronation,
    Yet now I must confess, that duty done,
    My thoughts and wishes bend again toward France   55
    And bow them to your gracious leave and pardon.

90

KING: Have you your father's leave? What says Polonius?
POLONIUS: H'ath, my lord, wrung from me my slow leave
    By laborsome petition, and at last
    Upon his will I sealed my hard consent.   60
    I do beseech you, give him leave to go.
KING: Take thy fair hour, Laertes. Time be thine,
    And thy best graces spend it at thy will!
    But now, my cousin Hamlet, and my son—
HAMLET: A little more than kin, and less than kind.   65
KING: How is that the clouds still hang on you?
HAMLET: Not so, my lord. I am too much in the sun.
QUEEN: Good Hamlet, cast thy nighted color off,
    And let thine eye look like a friend on Denmark.
    Do not forever with thy vailèd lids   · 70
    Seek for thy noble father in the dust.
    Thou know'st 'tis common, all that lives must die,
    Passing through nature to eternity.
HAMLET: Ay, madam, it is common.
QUEEN: If it be,
    Why seems it so particular with thee?   75
HAMLET: Seems, madam? Nay, it is. I know not "seems."
    'Tis not alone my inky cloak, good Mother,
    Nor customary suits of solemn black,
    Nor windy suspiration of forced breath,
    No, nor the fruitful river in the eye,   80
    Nor the dejected havior of the visage,
    Together with all forms, moods, shapes of grief,
    That can denote me truly. These indeed seem,
    For they are actions that a man might play.
    But I have that within which passes show;   85
    These but the trappings and the suits of woe.
KING: 'Tis sweet and commendable in your nature, Hamlet,
    To give these mourning duties to your father.
    But you must know your father lost a father,
    That father lost, lost his, and the survivor bound   90
    In filial obligation for some term
    To do obsequious sorrow. But to persever
    In obstinate condolement is a course
    Of impious stubbornness. 'Tis unmanly grief.
    It shows a will most incorrect to heaven,   95
    A heart unfortified, a mind impatient,
    An understanding simple and unschooled.
    For what we know must be and is as common
    As any the most vulgar thing to sense,
    Why should we in our peevish opposition   100
    Take it to heart? Fie, 'tis a fault to heaven,
    A fault against the dead, a fault to nature,
    To reason most absurd, whose common theme

Is death of fathers, and who still hath cried,
From the first corpse till he that died today,   105
"This must be so." We pray you, throw to earth
This unprevailing woe and think of us
As of a father; for let the world take note,
You are the most immediate to our throne,
And with no less nobility of love   110
Than that which dearest father bears his son
Do I impart toward you. For your intent
In going back to school in Wittenberg,
It is most retrograde to our desire,
And we beseech you bend you to remain   115
Here in the cheer and comfort of our eye,
Our chiefest courtier, cousin, and our son.
QUEEN: Let not thy mother lose her prayers, Hamlet.
   I pray thee, stay with us, go not to Wittenberg.
HAMLET: I shall in all my best obey you, madam.   120
KING: Why, 'tis a loving and a fair reply.
   Be as ourself in Denmark. Madam, come.
   This gentle and unforced accord of Hamlet
   Sits smiling to my heart, in grace whereof
   No jocund health that Denmark drinks today   125
   But the great cannon to the clouds shall tell,
   And the King's rouse the heaven shall bruit again,
   Respeaking earthly thunder. Come away.

Flourish. Exeunt all but Hamlet.

HAMLET: O, that this too too sullied flesh would melt,
   Thaw, and resolve itself into a dew!   130
   Or that the Everlasting had not fixed
   His canon 'gainst self-slaughter! O God, God,
   How weary, stale, flat, and unprofitable
   Seem to me all the uses of this world!
   Fie on 't, ah fie! 'Tis an unweeded garden   135
   That grows to seed. Things rank and gross in nature
   Possess it merely. That it should come to this!
   But two months dead—nay, not so much, not two.
   So excellent a king, that was to this
   Hyperion to a satyr, so loving to my mother   140
   That he might not beteem the winds of heaven
   Visit her face too roughly. Heaven and earth,
   Must I remember? Why, she would hang on him
   As if increase of appetite had grown
   By what it fed on, and yet within a month—   145
   Let me not think on 't; frailty, thy name is woman!—
   A little month, or ere those shoes were old
   With which she followed my poor father's body,

Like Niobe, all tears, why she, even she—
O God, a beast, that wants discourse of reason,   150
Would have mourned longer—married with my uncle,
My father's brother, but no more like my father
Than I to Hercules. Within a month,
Ere yet the salt of most unrighteous tears
Had left the flushing in her gallèd eyes,   155
She married. O, most wicked speed, to post
With such dexterity to incestuous sheets!
It is not, nor it cannot come to good.
But break, my heart, for I must hold my tongue.

Enter Horatio, Marcellus, and Bernardo.

HORATIO: Hail to your lordship!   160
HAMLET: I am glad to see you well.
    Horatio!—or I do forget myself.
HORATIO: The same, my lord, and your poor servant ever.
HAMLET: Sir, my good friend; I'll change that name with you.
    And what make you from Wittenberg, Horatio?—
    Marcellus.   165
MARCELLUS: My good lord.
HAMLET: I am very glad to see you. [*To Bernardo.*] Good even, sir.—
    But what in faith make you from Wittenberg?
HORATIO: A truant disposition, good my lord.
HAMLET: I would not hear your enemy say so,   170
    Nor shall you do my ear that violence
    To make it truster of your own report
    Against yourself. I know you are no truant.
    But what is your affair in Elsinore?
    We'll teach you to drink deep ere you depart.   175
HORATIO: My lord, I came to see your father's funeral.
HAMLET: I prithee, do not mock me, fellow student;
    I think it was to see my mother's wedding.
HORATIO: Indeed, my lord, it followed hard upon.
HAMLET: Thrift, thrift, Horatio! The funeral baked meats   180
    Did coldly furnish forth the marriage tables.
    Would I had met my dearest foe in heaven
    Or ever I had seen that day, Horatio!
    My father!—Methinks I see my father.
HORATIO: Where, my lord?
HAMLET: In my mind's eye, Horatio.   185
HORATIO: I saw him once. 'A was a goodly king.
HAMLET: 'A was a man. Take him for all in all,
    I shall not look upon his like again.
HORATIO: My lord, I think I saw him yesternight.
HAMLET: Saw? Who?   190
HORATIO: My lord, the King your father.

HAMLET: The King my father?

HORATIO: Season your admiration for a while
With an attent ear till I may deliver,
Upon the witness of these gentlemen,   195
This marvel to you.

HAMLET: For God's love, let me hear!

HORATIO: Two nights together had these gentlemen,
Marcellus and Bernardo, on their watch,
In the dead waste and middle of the night,
Been thus encountered. A figure like your father,   200
Armèd at point exactly, cap-à-pie,
Appears before them, and with solemn march
Goes slow and stately by them. Thrice he walked
By their oppressed and fear-surprisèd eyes
Within his truncheon's length, whilst they, distilled 205
Almost to jelly with the act of fear,
Stand dumb and speak not to him. This to me
In dreadful secrecy impart they did,
And I with them the third night kept the watch,
Where, as they had delivered, both in time,   210
Form of the thing, each word made true and good,
The apparition comes. I knew your father;
These hands are not more like.

HAMLET: But where was this?

MARCELLUS: My lord, upon the platform where we watch.

HAMLET: Did you not speak to it?

HORATIO: My lord, I did,   215
But answer made it none. Yet once methought
It lifted up its head and did address
Itself to motion, like as it would speak;
But even then the morning cock crew loud,
And at the sound it shrunk in haste away   220
And vanished from our sight.

HAMLET: 'Tis very strange.

HORATIO: As I do live, my honored lord, 'tis true,
And we did think it writ down in our duty
To let you know of it.

HAMLET: Indeed, indeed sirs. But this troubles me.   225
Hold you the watch tonight?

ALL: We do, my lord.

HAMLET: Armed, say you?

ALL: Armed, my lord.

HAMLET: From top to toe?

ALL: My lord, from head to foot.   230

HAMLET: Then saw you not his face?

HORATIO: O, yes my lord, he wore his beaver up.

HAMLET: What looked he, frowningly?

HORATIO: A countenance more in sorrow than in anger.

HAMLET: Pale or red? 235
HORATIO: Nay, very pale.
HAMLET: And fixed his eyes upon you?
HORATIO: Most constantly.
HAMLET: I would I had been there.
HORATIO: It would have much amazed you. 240
HAMLET: Very like, very like. Stayed it long?
HORATIO: While one with moderate haste might tell a hundred.
MARCELLUS, BERNARDO: Longer, longer.
HORATIO: Not when I saw 't.
HAMLET: His beard was grizzled—no? 245
HORATIO: It was, as I have seen it in his life,
    A sable silvered.
HAMLET: I will watch tonight.
    Perchance 'twill walk again.
HORATIO: I warrant it will.
HAMLET: If it assume my noble father's person,
    I'll speak to it though hell itself should gape 250
    And bid me hold my peace. I pray you all,
    If you have hitherto concealed this sight,
    Let it be tenable in your silence still,
    And whatsoever else shall hap tonight,
    Give it an understanding but no tongue. 255
    I will requite your loves. So, fare you well.
    Upon the platform twixt eleven and twelve
    I'll visit you.
ALL: Our duty to your honor.
HAMLET: Your loves, as mine to you. Farewell.

Exeunt all but Hamlet.

My father's spirit in arms! All is not well. 260
I doubt some foul play. Would the night were come!
Till then sit still, my soul. Foul deeds will rise,
Though all the earth o'erwhelm them, to men's eyes.

Exit.

ACT I. SCENE III

Enter Laertes and Ophelia, his sister.

LAERTES: My necessaries are embarked. Farewell.
    And, sister, as the winds give benefit
    And convoy is assistant, do not sleep
    But let me hear from you.
OPHELIA: Do you doubt that?
LAERTES: For Hamlet, and the trifling of his favor, 5

Hold it a fashion and a toy in blood,
A violet in the youth of primy nature,
Forward, not permanent, sweet, not lasting,
The perfume and suppliance of a minute—
No more.
OPHELIA: No more but so?
LAERTES: Think it no more.   10
   For nature crescent does not grow alone
   In thews and bulk, but as this temple waxes
   The inward service of the mind and soul
   Grows wide withal. Perhaps he loves you now,
   And now no soil nor cautel doth besmirch   15
   The virtue of his will; but you must fear,
   His greatness weighed, his will is not his own.
   For he himself is subject to his birth.
   He may not, as unvalued persons do,
   Carve for himself, for on his choice depends   20
   The safety and health of this whole state,
   And therefore must his choice be circumscribed
   Unto the voice and yielding of that body
   Whereof he is the head. Then if he says he loves you,
   It fits your wisdom so far to believe it   25
   As he in his particular act and place
   May give his saying deed, which is no further
   Than the main voice of Denmark goes withal.
   Then weigh what loss your honor may sustain
   If with too credent ear you list his songs,   30
   Or lose your heart, or your chaste treasure open
   To his unmastered importunity.
   Fear it, Ophelia, fear it, my dear sister,
   And keep you in the rear of your affection,
   Out of the shot and danger of desire.   35
   The chariest maid is prodigal enough
   If she unmask her beauty to the moon.
   Virtue itself scapes not calumnious strokes.
   The canker galls the infants of the spring
   Too oft before their buttons be disclosed,   40
   And in the morn and liquid dew of youth
   Contagious blastments are most imminent.
   Be wary then; best safety lies in fear.
   Youth to itself rebels, though none else near.
OPHELIA: I shall the effect of this good lesson keep   45
   As watchman to my heart. But, good my brother,
   Do not, as some ungracious pastors do,
   Show me the steep and thorny way to heaven,
   Whiles like a puffed and reckless libertine
   Himself the primrose path of dalliance treads,   50
   And recks not his own rede.

Enter Polonius.

LAERTES: O, fear me not.
    I stay too long. But here my father comes.
    A double blessing is a double grace;
    Occasion smiles upon a second leave.
POLONIUS: Yet here, Laertes? Aboard, aboard, for shame!   55
    The wind sits in the shoulder of your sail,
    And you are stayed for. There—my blessing with thee!
    And these few precepts in thy memory
    Look thou character. Give thy thoughts no tongue,
    Nor any unproportioned thought his act.   60
    Be thou familiar, but by no means vulgar.
    Those friends thou hast, and their adoption tried,
    Grapple them unto thy soul with hoops of steel,
    But do not dull thy palm with entertainment
    Of each new-hatched, unfledged courage. Beware   65
    Of entrance to a quarrel, but being in,
    Bear 't that th' opposèd may beware of thee.
    Give every man thy ear, but few thy voice;
    Take each man's censure, but reserve thy judgment.
    Costly thy habit as thy purse can buy,   70
    But not expressed in fancy; rich, not gaudy,
    For the apparel oft proclaims the man,
    And they in France of the best rank and station
    Are of a most select and generous chief in that.
    Neither a borrower nor a lender be;   75
    For loan oft loses both itself and friend,
    And borrowing dulls the edge of husbandry.
    This above all: to thine own self be true,
    And it must follow, as the night the day,
    Thou canst not then be false to any man.   80
    Farewell. My blessing season this in thee!
LAERTES: Most humbly do I take my leave, my lord.
POLONIUS: The time invests you. Go, your servants tend.
LAERTES: Farewell, Ophelia, and remember well
    What I have said to you.   85
OPHELIA: 'Tis in my memory locked,
    And you yourself shall keep the key of it.
LAERTES: Farewell.

Exit Laertes.

POLONIUS: What is 't, Ophelia, he hath said to you?
OPHELIA: So please you, something touching the Lord Hamlet.   90
POLONIUS: Marry, well bethought.
    'Tis told me he hath very oft of late
    Given private time to you, and you yourself

97

Have of your audience been most free and bounteous.
If it be so—as so 'tis put on me,   95
And that in way of caution—I must tell you
You do not understand yourself so clearly
As it behooves my daughter and your honor.
What is between you? Give me up the truth.
OPHELIA: He hath, my lord, of late made many tenders   100
Of his affection to me.
POLONIUS: Affection? Pooh! You speak like a green girl,
Unsifted in such perilous circumstance.
Do you believe his tenders, as you call them?
OPHELIA: I do not know, my lord, what I should think.   105
POLONIUS: Marry, I will teach you. Think yourself a baby
That you have ta'en these tenders for true pay
Which are not sterling. Tender yourself more dearly,
Or—not to crack the wind of the poor phrase,
Running it thus—you'll tender me a fool.   110
OPHELIA: My lord, he hath importuned me with love
In honorable fashion.
POLONIUS: Ay, fashion you may call it. Go to, go to.
OPHELIA: And hath given countenance to his speech, my lord,
With almost all the holy vows of heaven.   115
POLONIUS: Ay, springes to catch woodcocks. I do know,
When the blood burns, how prodigal the soul
Lends the tongue vows. These blazes, daughter,
Giving more light than heat, extinct in both
Even in their promise as it is a-making.   120
You must not take for fire. From this time
Be something scanter of your maiden presence.
Set your entreatments at a higher rate
Than a command to parle. For Lord Hamlet,
Believe so much in him that he is young,   125
And with a larger tether may he walk
Than may be given you. In few, Ophelia,
Do not believe his vows, for they are brokers,
Not of that dye which their investments show,
But mere implorators of unholy suits,   130
Breathing like sanctified and pious bawds
The better to beguile. This is for all:
I would not, in plain terms, from this time forth
Have you so slander any moment leisure
As to give words or talk with the Lord Hamlet.   135
Look to 't, I charge you. Come your ways.
OPHELIA: I shall obey, my lord.

Exeunt.

98

ACT I. SCENE IV

Enter Hamlet, Horatio, and Marcellus.

HAMLET: The air bites shrewdly; it is very cold.
HORATIO: It is a nipping and an eager air.
HAMLET: What hour now?
HORATIO: I think it lacks of twelve.
MARCELLUS: No, it is struck.
HORATIO: Indeed? I heard it not.
    It then draws near the season   5
    Wherein the spirit held his wont to walk.

            A flourish of trumpets, and two pieces go off [within].

    What does this mean, my lord?
HAMLET: The King doth wake tonight and takes his rouse,
    Keeps wassail, and the swaggering upspring reels;
    And as he drains his drafts of Rhenish down,   10
    The kettledrum and trumpet thus bray out
    The triumph of his pledge.
HORATIO: Is it a custom?
HAMLET: Ay, marry, is't,
    But to my mind, though I am native here
    And to the manner born, it is a custom   15
    More honored in the breach than the observance.
    This heavy-headed revel east and west
    Makes us traduced and taxed of other nations.
    They clepe us drunkards, and with swinish phrase
    Soil our addition; and indeed it takes   20
    From our achievements, though performed at height,
    The pith and marrow of our attribute.
    So, oft it chances in particular men,
    That for some vicious mole of nature in them,
    As in their birth—wherein they are not guilty.   25
    Since nature cannot choose his origin—
    By their o'ergrowth of some complexion,
    Oft breaking down the pales and forts of reason,
    Or by some habit that too much o'erleavens
    The form of plausive manners, that these men,   30
    Carrying, I say, the stamp of one defect,
    Being nature's livery or fortune's star,
    His virtues else, be they as pure as grace,
    As infinite as man may undergo,
    Shall in the general censure take corruption   35
    From that particular fault. The dram of evil
    Doth all the noble substance often dout
    To his own scandal.

Enter Ghost.

HORATIO: Look, my lord, it comes!
HAMLET: Angels and ministers of grace defend us!
    Be thou a spirit of health or goblin damned,   40
    Bring with thee airs from heaven or blasts from hell,
    Be thy intents wicked or charitable,
    Thou com'st in such a questionable shape
    That I will speak to thee. I'll call thee Hamlet,
    King, Father, royal Dane. O, answer me!   45
    Let me not burst in ignorance, but tell
    Why thy canonized bones, hearsèd in death,
    Have burst their cerements; why the sepulcher
    Wherein we saw thee quietly inurned
    Hath oped his ponderous and marble jaws   50
    To cast thee up again. What may this mean,
    That thou, dead corpse, again in complete steel,
    Revisits thus the glimpses of the moon,
    Making night hideous, and we fools of nature
    So horridly to shake our disposition   55
    With thoughts beyond the reaches of our souls?
    Say, why is this? Wherefore? What should we do?

The Ghost beckons Hamlet.

HORATIO: It beckons you to go away with it.
    As if it some impartment did desire
    To you alone.
MARCELLUS: Look with what courteous action   60
    It wafts you to a more removèd ground.
    But do not go with it.
HORATIO: No, by no means.
HAMLET: It will not speak. Then I will follow it.
HORATIO: Do not, my lord!
HAMLET: Why, what should be the fear?
    I do not set my life at a pin's fee,   65
    And for my soul, what can it do to that,
    Being a thing immortal as itself?
    It waves me forth again. I'll follow it.
HORATIO: What if it tempt you toward the flood, my lord,
    Or to the dreadful summit of the cliff   70
    That beetles o'er his base into the sea,
    And there assume some other horrible form
    Which might deprive your sovereignty of reason
    And draw you into madness? Think of it.
    The very place puts toys of desperation,   75
    Without more motive, into every brain

That looks so many fathoms to the sea
And hears its roar beneath.
HAMLET: It wafts me still.—Go on, I'll follow thee.
MARCELLUS: You shall not go, my lord.

[They try to stop him.]

HAMLET: Hold off your hands!   80
HORATIO: Be ruled. You shall not go.
HAMLET: My fate cries out,
    And makes each petty artery in this body
    As hardy as the Nemean lion's nerve.
    Still am I called. Unhand me, gentlemen.
    By heaven, I'll make a ghost of him that lets me!   85
    I say, away!—Go on, I'll follow thee.

Exeunt Ghost and Hamlet.

HORATIO: He waxes desperate with imagination.
MARCELLUS: Let's follow. 'Tis not fit thus to obey him.
HORATIO: Have after. To what issue will this come?
MARCELLUS: Something is rotten in the state of Denmark.   90
HORATIO: Heaven will direct it.
MARCELLUS: Nay, let's follow him.

Exeunt.

ACT I. SCENE V

Enter Ghost and Hamlet.

HAMLET: Whither wilt thou lead me? Speak. I'll go no further.
GHOST: Mark me.
HAMLET: I will.
GHOST: My hour is almost come,
    When I to sulfurous and tormenting flames
    Must render up myself.
HAMLET: Alas, poor ghost!
GHOST: Pity me not, but lend thy serious hearing   5
    To what I shall unfold.
HAMLET: Speak. I am bound to hear.
GHOST: So art thou to revenge, when thou shalt hear.
HAMLET: What?
GHOST: I am thy father's spirit,   10
    Doomed for a certain term to walk the night,
    And for the day confined to fast in fires,
    Till the foul crimes done in my days of nature

101

Are burnt and purged away. But that I am forbid
To tell the secrets of my prison house,   15
I could a tale unfold whose lightest word
Would harrow up thy soul, freeze thy young blood,
Make thy two eyes like stars start from their spheres,
Thy knotted and combinèd locks to part,
And each particular hair to stand on end   20
Like quills upon the fretful porpentine.
But this eternal blazon must not be
To ears of flesh and blood. List, list, O, list!
If thou didst ever thy dear father love—
HAMLET: O God!   25
GHOST: Revenge his foul and most unnatural murder.
HAMLET: Murder?
GHOST: Murder most foul, as in the best it is,
    But this most foul, strange, and unnatural.
HAMLET: Haste me to know 't, that I, with wings as swift   30
    As meditation or the thoughts of love
    May sweep to my revenge.
GHOST: I find thee apt;
    And duller shouldst thou be than the fat weed
    That roots itself in ease on Lethe wharf,
    Wouldst thou not stir in this. Now, Hamlet, hear.   35
    'Tis given out that, sleeping in my orchard,
    A serpent stung me. So the whole ear of Denmark
    Is by a forgèd process of my death
    Rankly abused. But know, thou noble youth,
    The serpent that did sting thy father's life   40
    Now wears his crown.
HAMLET: O, my prophetic soul! My uncle!
GHOST: Ay, that incestuous, that adulterate beast,
    With witchcraft of his wit, with traitorous gifts—
    O wicked wit and gifts, that have the power   45
    So to seduce!—won to his shameful lust
    The will of my most seeming-virtuous queen.
    O Hamlet, what a falling off was there!
    From me, whose love was of that dignity
    That it went hand in hand even with the vow   50
    I made to her in marriage, and to decline
    Upon a wretch whose natural gifts were poor
    To those of mine!
    But virtue, as it never will be moved,
    Though lewdness court it in a shape of heaven,   55
    So lust, though to a radiant angel linked,
    Will sate itself in a celestial bed
    And prey on garbage.
    But soft, methinks I scent the morning air.
    Brief let me be. Sleeping within my orchard,   60

My custom always of the afternoon,
Upon my secure hour thy uncle stole,
With juice of cursèd hebona in a vial,
And in the porches of my ears did pour
The leprous distillment, whose effect   65
Holds such an enmity with blood of man
That swift as quicksilver it courses through
The natural gates and alleys of the body,
And with a sudden vigor it doth posset
And curd, like eager droppings into milk,   70
The thin and wholesome blood. So did it mine,
And a most instant tetter barked about,
Most lazar-like, with vile and loathsome crust,
All my smooth body.
Thus was I, sleeping, by a brother's hand   75
Of life, of crown, of queen at once dispatched,
Cut off even in the blossoms of my sin,
Unhouseled, disappointed, unaneled,
No reckoning made, but sent to my account
With all my imperfections on my head.   80
O, horrible! O, horrible, most horrible!
If thou hast nature in thee, bear it not.
Let not the royal bed of Denmark be
A couch for luxury and damnèd incest.
But, howsoever thou pursues this act,   85
Taint not thy mind nor let thy soul contrive
Against thy mother aught. Leave her to heaven
And to those thorns that in her bosom lodge,
To prick and sting her. Fare thee well at once.
The glowworm shows the matin to be near,   90
And 'gins to pale his uneffectual fire.
Adieu, adieu, adieu! Remember me.

                                                                        Exit.

HAMLET: O all you host of heaven! O earth! What else?
    And shall I couple hell? O, fie! Hold, hold, my heart,
    And you, my sinews, grow not instant old,   95
    But bear me stiffly up. Remember thee?
    Ay, thou poor ghost, whiles memory holds a seat
    In this distracted globe. Remember thee?
    Yea, from the table of my memory
    I'll wipe away all trivial fond records,   100
    All saws of books, all forms, all pressures past
    That youth and observation copied there,
    And thy commandment all alone shall live
    Within the book and volume of my brain,
    Unmixed with baser matter. Yes, by heaven!   105

                                103

O most pernicious woman!
O villain, villain, smiling, damnèd villain!
My tables—meet it is I set it down
That one may smile, and smile, and be a villain.
At least I am sure it may be so in Denmark.   110

                                                              [*Writing.*]

So, uncle, there you are. Now to my word:
It is "Adieu, adieu! Remember me."
I have sworn 't.

Enter Horatio and Marcellus.

HORATIO: My lord, my lord!
MARCELLUS: Lord Hamlet!   115
HORATIO: Heavens secure him!
HAMLET: So be it.
MARCELLUS: Hillo, ho, ho, my lord!
HAMLET: Hillo, ho, ho, boy! Come, bird, come.
MARCELLUS: How is 't, my noble lord?   120
HORATIO: What news, my lord?
HAMLET: O, wonderful!
HORATIO: Good my lord, tell it.
HAMLET: No, you will reveal it.
HORATIO: Not I, my lord, by heaven.   125
MARCELLUS: Nor I, my lord.
HAMLET: How say you, then, would heart of man once think it?
     But you'll be secret?
HORATIO, MARCELLUS: Ay, by heaven, my lord.
HAMLET: There's never a villain dwelling in all Denmark
     But he's an arrant knave.   130
HORATIO: There needs no ghost, my lord, come from the grave
     To tell us this.
HAMLET: Why, right, you are in the right.
     And so, without more circumstance at all,
     I hold it fit that we shake hands and part,
     You as your business and desire shall point you—   135
     For every man hath business and desire,
     Such as it is—and for my own poor part,
     Look you, I'll go pray.
HORATIO: These are but wild and whirling words, my lord.
HAMLET: I am sorry they offend you, heartily;   140
     Yes, faith, heartily.
HORATIO: There's no offense, my lord.
HAMLET: Yes, by Saint Patrick, but there is, Horatio.
     And much offense too. Touching this vision here,
     It is an honest ghost, that let me tell you.

For your desire to know what is between us,   145
O'ermaster 't as you may. And now, good friends,
As you are friends, scholars, and soldiers,
Give me one poor request.
HORATIO: What is 't, my lord? We will.
HAMLET: Never make known what you have seen tonight.   150
HORATIO, MARCELLUS: My lord, we will not.
HAMLET: Nay, but swear 't.
HORATIO: In faith, my lord, not I.
MARCELLUS: Nor I, my lord, in faith.
HAMLET: Upon my sword. [*He holds out his sword.*]   155
MARCELLUS: We have sworn, my lord, already.
HAMLET: Indeed, upon my sword, indeed.
GHOST: (*Cries under the stage*) Swear.
HAMLET: Ha, ha, boy, sayst thou so? Art thou there, truepenny?
   Come on, you hear this fellow in the cellerage.   160
   Consent to swear.
HORATIO: Propose the oath, my lord.
HAMLET: Never to speak of this that you have seen,
   Swear by my sword.
GHOST: [*Beneath*] Swear.

                                             [*They swear.*]

HAMLET: *Hic et ubique?* Then we'll shift our ground.   165

                                  [*He moves to another spot.*]

   Come hither, gentlemen,
   And lay your hands again upon my sword.
   Swear by my sword
   Never to speak of this that you have heard.
GHOST: [*Beneath*] Swear by his sword.   170

                                             [*They swear.*]

HAMLET: Well said, old mole. Canst work i' th' earth so fast?
   A worthy pioneer! Once more remove, good friends.

                                          [*He moves again.*]

HORATIO: O day and night, but this is wondrous strange!
HAMLET: And therefore as a stranger give it welcome.
   There are more things in heaven and earth, Horatio,   175
   Than are dreamt of in your philosophy.
   But come;
   Here, as before, never, so help you mercy,
   How strange or odd soe'er I bear myself—

As I perchance hereafter shall think meet   180
    To put an antic disposition on—
    That you, at such times seeing me, never shall,
    With arms encumbered thus, or this headshake,
    Or by pronouncing of some doubtful phrase
    As "Well, we know," or "We could, an if we would,"   185
    Or "If we list to speak," or "There be, an if they might,"
    Or such ambiguous giving out, to note
    That you know aught of me—this do swear,
    So grace and mercy at your most need help you.
GHOST: [Beneath] Swear.   190

                                                            [They swear.]

HAMLET: Rest, rest, perturbèd spirit! So, gentlemen,
    With all my love I do commend me to you;
    And what so poor a man as Hamlet is
    May do t' express his love and friending to you,
    God willing, shall not lack. Let us go in together,   195
    And still your fingers on your lips, I pray.
    The time is out of joint. O cursèd spite
    That ever I was born to set it right!

                                        [They wait for him to leave first.]

    Nay, come, let's go together.

ACT II

SCENE I

Enter old Polonius with his man [Reynaldo].

POLONIUS: Give him this money and these notes, Reynaldo.

                                        [He gives money and papers.]

REYNALDO: I will, my lord.
POLONIUS: You shall do marvelous wisely, good Reynaldo,
    Before you visit him, to make inquire
    Of his behavior.
REYNALDO: My lord, I did intend it.   5
POLONIUS: Marry, well said, very well said. Look you, sir,
    Inquire me first what Danskers are in Paris,
    And how, and who, what means, and where they keep,
    What company, at what expense; and finding
    By this encompassment and drift of question   10
    That they do know my son, come you more nearer

Than your particular demands will touch it.
Take you, as 'twere, some distant knowledge of him,
As thus, "I know his father and his friends,
And in part him." Do you mark this, Reynaldo?   15
REYNALDO: Ay, very well, my lord.
POLONIUS: "And in part him, but," you may say, "not well.
But if 't be he I mean, he's very wild,
Addicted so and so," and there put on him
What forgeries you please—marry, none so rank   20
As may dishonor him, take heed of that,
But, sir, such wanton, wild, and usual slips
As are companions noted and most known
To youth and liberty.
REYNALDO: As gaming, my lord.   25
POLONIUS: Ay, or drinking, fencing, swearing,
Quarreling, drabbing—you may go so far.
REYNALDO: My lord, that would dishonor him.
POLONIUS: Faith, no, as you may season it in the charge.
You must not put another scandal on him   30
That he is open to incontinency;
That's not my meaning. But breathe his faults so
quaintly
That they may seem the taints of liberty,
The flash and outbreak of a fiery mind,
A savageness in unreclaimèd blood,   35
Of general assault.
REYNALDO: But, my good lord—
POLONIUS: Wherefore should you do this?
REYNALDO: Ay, my lord, I would know that.
POLONIUS: Marry, sir, here's my drift,   40
And I believe it is a fetch of warrant.
You laying these slight sullies on my son,
As 'twere a thing a little soiled wi' the working,
Mark you,
Your party in converse, him you would sound,   45
Having ever seen in the prenominate crimes
The youth you breathe of guilty, be assured
He closes with you in this consequence:
"Good sir," or so, or "friend," or "gentleman,"
According to the phrase or the addition   50
Of man and country.
REYNALDO: Very good, my lord.
POLONIUS: And then, sir, does 'a this—'a does—what was I
about to say? By the Mass, I was about to say something.
Where did I leave?
REYNALDO: At "closes in the consequence."   55
POLONIUS: At "closes in the consequence," ay, marry.
He closes thus: "I know the gentleman,

I saw him yesterday," or "th' other day,"
Or then, or then, with such or such, "and as you say,
There was 'a gaming," "there o'ertook in 's rouse,"   60
"There falling out at tennis," or perchance
"I saw him enter such a house of sale,"
Videlicet a brothel, or so forth. See you now,
Your bait of falsehood takes this carp of truth;
And thus do we of wisdom and of reach,   65
With windlasses and with assays of bias,
By indirections find directions out.
So by my former lecture and advice
Shall you my son. You have me, have you not?
REYNALDO: My lord, I have.
POLONIUS: God b' wi' ye; fare ye well.   70
REYNALDO: Good my lord.
POLONIUS: Observe his inclination in yourself.
REYNALDO: I shall, my lord.
POLONIUS: And let him ply his music.
REYNALDO: Well, my lord.   75
POLONIUS: Farewell.

Exit Reynaldo.

Enter Ophelia.

How now, Ophelia, what's the matter?
OPHELIA: O my lord, my lord, I have been so affrighted!
POLONIUS: With what, i' the name of God?
OPHELIA: My lord, as I was sewing in my closet,
Lord Hamlet, with his doublet all unbraced,   80
No hat upon his head, his stockings fouled,
Ungartered, and down-gyvèd to his ankle,
Pale as his shirt, his knees knocking each other,
And with a look so piteous in purport
As if he had been loosèd out of hell   85
To speak of horrors—he comes before me.
POLONIUS: Mad for thy love?
OPHELIA: My lord, I do not know,
But truly I do fear it.
POLONIUS: What said he?
OPHELIA: He took me by the wrist and held me hard.
Then goes he to the length of all his arm,   90
And with his other hand thus o'er his brow
He falls to such perusal of my face
As 'a would draw it. Long stayed he so.
At last, a little shaking of mine arm
And thrice his head thus waving up and down,   95
He raised a sigh so piteous and profound

108

As it did seem to shatter all his bulk
And end his being. That done, he lets me go,
And with his head over his shoulder turned
He seemed to find his way without his eyes,   100
For out o' doors he went without their helps,
And to the last bended their light on me.
POLONIUS: Come, go with me. I will go seek the King.
This is the very ecstasy of love,
Whose violent property fordoes itself   105
And leads the will to desperate undertakings
As oft as any passion under heaven
That does afflict our natures. I am sorry.
What, have you given him any hard words of late?
OPHELIA: No, my good lord, but as you did command   110
I did repel his letters and denied
His access to me.
POLONIUS: That hath made him mad.
I am sorry that with better heed and judgment
I had not quoted him. I feared he did but trifle
And meant to wrack thee. But beshrew my jealousy!   115
By heaven, it is as proper to our age
To cast beyond ourselves in our opinions
As it is common for the younger sort
To lack discretion. Come, go we to the King.
This must be known, which, being kept close, might
    move   120
More grief to hide than hate to utter love.
Come.

Exeunt.

ACT II. SCENE II

Flourish. Enter King and Queen, Rosencrantz, and Guildenstern [with others].

KING: Welcome, dear Rosencrantz and Guildenstern.
Moreover that we much did long to see you,
The need we have to use you did provoke
Our hasty sending. Something have you heard
Of Hamlet's transformation—so call it,   5
Sith nor th' exterior nor the inward man
Resembles that it was. What it should be,
More than his father's death, that thus hath put him
So much from th' understanding of himself,
I cannot dream of. I entreat you both   10
That, being of so young days brought up with him,
And sith so neighbored to his youth and havior,
That you vouchsafe your rest here in our court

109

Some little time, so by your companies
To draw him on to pleasures, and to gather   15
So much as from occasion you may glean,
Whether aught to us unknown afflicts him thus
That, opened, lies within our remedy.
QUEEN: Good gentlemen, he hath much talked of you,
And sure I am two men there is not living   20
To whom he more adheres. If it will please you
To show us so much gentry and good will
As to expend your time with us awhile
For the supply and profit of our hope,
Your visitation shall receive such thanks   25
As fits a king's remembrance.
ROSENCRANTZ: Both Your Majesties
Might, by the sovereign power you have of us,
Put your dread pleasures more into command
Than to entreaty.
GUILDENSTERN: But we both obey,
And here give up ourselves in the full bent   30
To lay our service freely at your feet,
To be commanded.
KING: Thanks, Rosencrantz and gentle Guildenstern.
QUEEN: Thanks, Guildenstern and gentle Rosencrantz.
And I beseech you instantly to visit   35
My too much changèd son. Go, some of you,
And bring these gentlemen where Hamlet is.
GUILDENSTERN: Heavens make our presence and our practices
Pleasant and helpful to him!
QUEEN: Ay, amen!

Exeunt Rosencrantz and Guildenstern [with some attendants].

Enter Polonius.

POLONIUS: Th' ambassadors from Norway, my good lord,   40
Are joyfully returned.
KING: Thou still hast been the father of good news.
POLONIUS: Have I, my lord? I assure my good liege
I hold my duty, as I hold my soul,
Both to my God and to my gracious king;   45
And I do think, or else this brain of mine
Hunts not the trail of policy so sure
As it hath used to do, that I have found
The very cause of Hamlet's lunacy.
KING: O, speak of that! That do I long to hear.   50
POLONIUS: Give first admittance to th' ambassadors.
My news shall be the fruit to that great feast.
KING: Thyself do grace to them and bring them in.

He tells me, my dear Gertrude, he hath found
The head and source of all your son's distemper.   55
QUEEN: I doubt it is no other but the main,
His father's death and our o'erhasty marriage.

Enter Ambassadors [Voltimand and Cornelius, with Polonius].

KING: Well, we shall sift him.—Welcome, my good friends!
Say, Voltimand, what from our brother Norway?
VOLTIMAND: Most fair return of greetings and desires.   60
Upon our first, he sent out to suppress
His nephew's levies, which to him appeared
To be a preparation 'gainst the Polack,
But, better looked into, he truly found
It was against Your Highness. Whereat grieved   65
That so his sickness, age, and impotence
Was falsely borne in hand, sends out arrests
On Fortinbras, which he, in brief, obeys,
Receives rebuke from Norway, and in fine
Makes vow before his uncle never more   70
To give th' assay of arms against Your Majesty.
Whereon old Norway, overcome with joy,
Gives him three thousand crowns in annual fee
And his commission to employ those soldiers,
So levied as before, against the Polack,   75
With an entreaty, herein further shown,

[Giving a paper]

That it might please you to give quiet pass
Through your dominions for this enterprise
On such regards of safety and allowance
As therein are set down.
KING: It likes us well,   80
And at our more considered time we'll read,
Answer, and think upon this business.
Meantime we thank you for your well-took labor.
Go to your rest; at night we'll feast together.
Most welcome home!

Exeunt Ambassadors.

POLONIUS: This business is well ended.   85
My liege, and madam, to expostulate
What majesty should be, what duty is,
Why day is day, night night, and time is time,

111

Were nothing but to waste night, day, and time.
Therefore, since brevity is the soul of wit,   90
And tediousness the limbs and outward flourishes,
I will be brief. Your noble son is mad.
Mad call I it, for, to define true madness,
What is 't but to be nothing else but mad?
But let that go.
QUEEN: More matter, with less art.   95
POLONIUS: Madam, I swear I use no art at all.
   That he's mad, 'tis true; 'tis true 'tis pity,
   And pity 'tis 'tis true—a foolish figure,
   But farewell it, for I will use no art.
   Mad let us grant him, then, and now remains   100
   That we find out the cause of this effect,
   Or rather say, the cause of this defect,
   For this effect defective comes by cause
   Thus it remains, and the remainder thus.
   Perpend.   105
   I have a daughter—have while she is mine—
   Who, in her duty and obedience, mark,
   Hath given me this. Now gather and surmise.
   [*He reads the letter.*] "To the celestial and my soul's idol,
      the most beautified Ophelia"—   110
   That's an ill phrase, a vile phrase; "beautified" is a vile
      phrase. But you shall hear. Thus:

                                                          [*He reads.*]

   "In her excellent white bosom, these, etc."
QUEEN: Came this from Hamlet to her?
POLONIUS: Good madam, stay awhile. I will be faithful.   115

                                                          [*He reads.*]

               "Doubt thou the stars are fire,
               Doubt that the sun doth move,
               Doubt truth to be a liar,
               But never doubt I love.

   O dear Ophelia, I am ill at these numbers. I have not   120
   art to reckon my groans. But that I love thee best, O
   most best, believe it. Adieu.
        Thine evermore, most dear lady, whilst this
           machine is to him, Hamlet."
   This in obedience hath my daughter shown me,   125
   And, more above, hath his solicitings,
   As they fell out by time, by means, and place,
   All given to mine ear.

KING: But how hath she
    Received his love?
POLONIUS: What do you think of me?
KING: As of a man faithful and honorable. 130
POLONIUS: I would fain prove so. But what might you think,
    When I had seen this hot love on the wing—
    As I perceived it, I must tell you that,
    Before my daughter told me—what might you,
    Or my dear Majesty your queen here, think, 135
    If I had played the desk or table book,
    Or given my heart a winking, mute and dumb,
    Or looked upon this love with idle sight?
    What might you think? No, I went round to work,
    And my young mistress thus I did bespeak: 140
    "Lord Hamlet is a prince out of thy star;
    This must not be." And then I prescripts gave her
    That she should lock herself from his resort,
    Admit no messengers, receive no tokens.
    Which done, she took the fruits of my advice; 145
    And he, repellèd—a short tale to make—
    Fell into a sadness, then into a fast,
    Thence to a watch, thence into a weakness,
    Thence to a lightness, and by this declension
    Into the madness wherein now he raves 150
    And all we mourn for.
KING: [To Queen] Do you think 'tis this?
QUEEN: It may be, very like.
POLONIUS: Hath there been such a time—I would fain know that—
    That I have positively said "'Tis so,"
    When it proved otherwise?
KING: Not that I know. 155
POLONIUS: Take this from this, if this be otherwise.
    If circumstances lead me, I will find
    Where truth is hid, though it were hid indeed
    Within the center.
KING: How may we try it further?
POLONIUS: You know sometimes he walks four hours together 160
    Here in the lobby.
QUEEN: So he does indeed.
POLONIUS: At such a time I'll loose my daughter to him.
    Be you and I behind an arras then.
    Mark the encounter. If he love her not
    And be not from his reason fallen thereon, 165
    Let me be no assistant for a state,
    But keep a farm and carters.
KING: We will try it.

Enter Hamlet [reading on a book].

QUEEN: But look where sadly the poor wretch comes reading.
POLONIUS: Away, I do beseech you both, away.
    I'll board him presently. O, give me leave. 170

Exeunt King and Queen [with attendants].

    How does my good Lord Hamlet?
HAMLET: Well, God-a-mercy.
POLONIUS: Do you know me, my Lord?
HAMLET: Excellent well. You are a fishmonger.
POLONIUS: Not I, my lord. 175
HAMLET: Then I would you were so honest a man.
POLONIUS: Honest, my lord?
HAMLET: Ay, sir. To be honest, as this world goes, is to
    be one man picked out of ten thousand.
POLONIUS: That's very true, my lord. 180
HAMLET: For if the sun breed maggots in a dead dog,
    being a good kissing carrion—Have you a daughter?
POLONIUS: I have, my lord.
HAMLET: Let her not walk i' the sun. Conception is a
    blessing, but as your daughter may conceive, friend, 185
    look to 't.
POLONIUS: [*Aside*] How say you by that? Still harping
    on my daughter. Yet he knew me not at first; 'a said I
    was a fishmonger. 'A is far gone. And truly in my
    youth I suffered much extremity for love, very near 190
    this. I'll speak to him again.—What do you read, my
    lord?
HAMLET: Words, words, words.
POLONIUS: What is the matter, my lord?
HAMLET: Between who? 195
POLONIUS: I mean, the matter that you read, my lord.
HAMLET: Slanders, sir; for the satirical rogue says here
    that old men have gray beards, that their faces are wrinkled,
    their eyes purging thick amber and plum-tree
    gum, and that they have a plentiful lack of wit, 200
    together with most weak hams. All which, sir, though I
    most powerfully and potently believe, yet I hold it not
    honesty to have it thus set down, for yourself, sir, shall
    grow old as I am, if like a crab you could go backward.
POLONIUS: [*Aside*] Though this be madness, yet there is 205
    method in 't.—Will you walk out of the air, my lord?
HAMLET: Into my grave.
POLONIUS: Indeed, that's out of the air. [*Aside.*] How
    pregnant sometimes his replies are! A happiness that
    often madness hits on, which reason and sanity could 210
    not so prosperously be delivered of. I will leave him

and suddenly contrive the means of meeting between
him and my daughter.—My honorable lord, I will
most humbly take my leave of you.

HAMLET: You cannot, sir, take from me anything that I   215
    will more willingly part withal—except
    my life, except my life, except my life.

Enter Guildenstern and Rosencrantz.

POLONIUS: Fare you well, my lord.
HAMLET: These tedious old fools!
POLONIUS: You go to seek the Lord Hamlet. There he is.   220
ROSENCRANTZ: [*To Polonius*] God save you, sir!

Exit Polonius.

GUILDENSTERN: My honored lord!
ROSENCRANTZ: My most dear lord!
HAMLET: My excellent good friends! How dost thou, Guildenstern?
    Ah, Rosencrantz! Good lads, how do   225
    you both?
ROSENCRANTZ: As the indifferent children of the earth.
GUILDENSTERN: Happy in that we are not overhappy.
    On Fortune's cap we are not the very button.
HAMLET: Nor the soles of her shoe?   230
ROSENCRANTZ: Neither, my lord.
HAMLET: Then you live about her waist, or in the middle
    of her favors?
GUILDENSTERN: Faith, her privates we.
HAMLET: In the secret parts of Fortune? O, most true,   235
    she is a strumpet. What news?
ROSENCRANTZ: None, my lord, but the world's grown
    honest.
HAMLET: Then is doomsday near. But your news is not
    true. Let me question more in particular. What have   240
    you, my good friends, deserved at the hands of
    Fortune that she sends you to prison hither?
GUILDENSTERN: Prison, my lord?
HAMLET: Denmark's a prison.
ROSENCRANTZ: Then is the world one.   245
HAMLET: A goodly one, in which there are many
    confines, wards, and dungeons, Denmark being one
    o' the worst.
ROSENCRANTZ: We think not so, my lord.
HAMLET: Why then 'tis none to you, for there is nothing   250
    either good or bad but thinking makes it so. To me it
    is a prison.

ROSENCRANTZ: Why then, your ambition makes it one.
'Tis too narrow for your mind.

HAMLET: O God, I could be bounded in a nutshell and   255
count myself a king of infinite space, were it not that
I have bad dreams.

GUILDENSTERN: Which dreams indeed are ambition, for
the very substance of the ambitious is merely the
shadow of a dream.   260

HAMLET: A dream itself is but a shadow.

ROSENCRANTZ: Truly, and I hold ambition of so airy and
light a quality that it is but a shadow's shadow.

HAMLET: Then are our beggars bodies, and our mon-
archs and outstretched heroes the beggars' shadows.   265
Shall we to the court? For, by my fay, I cannot reason.

ROSENCRANTZ, GUILDENSTERN: We'll wait upon you.

HAMLET: No such matter. I will not sort you with the
rest of my servants, for, to speak to you like an honest
man, I am most dreadfully attended. But, in the   270
beaten way of friendship, what make you at Elsinore?

ROSENCRANTZ: To visit you, my lord, no other occasion.

HAMLET: Beggar that I am, I am even poor in thanks;
but I thank you, and sure, dear friends, my thanks are
too dear a halfpenny. Were you not sent for? Is it your   275
own inclining? Is it a free visitation? Come, come, deal
justly with me. Come, come; nay, speak.

GUILDENSTERN: What should we say, my lord?

HAMLET: Anything but to the purpose. You were sent
for, and there is a kind of confession in your looks which   280
your modesties have not craft enough to color. I know
the good King and Queen have sent for you.

ROSENCRANTZ: To what end, my lord?

HAMLET: That you must teach me. But let me conjure
you, by the rights of our fellowship, by the conso-   285
nancy of our youth, by the obligation of our ever-
preserved love, and by what more dear a better proposer
could charge you withal, be even and direct with me
whether you were sent for or no.

ROSENCRANTZ: [Aside to Guildenstern] What say you?

HAMLET: [Aside] Nay, then, I have an eye of you.—If   290
you love me, hold not off.

GUILDENSTERN: My lord, we were sent for.

HAMLET: I will tell you why; so shall my anticipation
prevent your discovery, and your secrecy to the King   295
and Queen molt no feather. I have of late—but
wherefore I know not—lost all my mirth, forgone all
custom of exercises; and indeed it goes so heavily with
my disposition that this goodly frame, the earth,
seems to me a sterile promontory; this most excellent   300

canopy, the air, look you, this brave o'erhanging fir-
mament, this majestical roof fretted with golden fire,
why, it appeareth nothing to me but a foul and pestilent congregation of vapors. What a piece of work is a
man! How noble in reason, how infinite in faculties,   305
in form and moving how express and admirable, in
action how like an angel, in apprehension how like a
god! The beauty of the world, the paragon of animals!
And yet, to me, what is this quintessence of dust?
Man delights not me—no, nor woman neither,   310
though by your smiling you seem to say so.
ROSENCRANTZ: My lord, there was no such stuff in my
thoughts.
HAMLET: Why did you laugh then, when I said man
delights not me?   315
ROSENCRANTZ: To think, my lord, if you delight not in
man, what Lenten entertainment the players shall receive from you. We coted them on the way, and hither
are they coming to offer you service.
HAMLET: He that plays the king shall be welcome; His   320
Majesty shall have tribute of me. The adventurous
knight shall use his foil and target, the lover shall not
sigh gratis, the humorous man shall end his part in
peace, the clown shall make those laugh whose lungs
are tickle o' the sear, and the lady shall say her mind   325
freely, or the blank verse shall halt for 't. What players
are they?
ROSENCRANTZ: Even those you were wont to take such
delight in, the tragedians of the city.
HAMLET: How chances it they travel? Their residence,   330
both in reputation and profit, was better both ways.
ROSENCRANTZ: I think their inhibition comes by the
means of the late innovation.
HAMLET: Do they hold the same estimation they did
when I was in the city? Are they so followed?   335
ROSENCRANTZ: No, indeed are they not.
HAMLET: How comes it? Do they grow rusty?
ROSENCRANTZ: Nay, their endeavor keeps in the wonted
pace. But there is, sir, an aerie of children, little eyases,
that cry out on the top of question and are most tyran-   340
nically clapped for 't. These are now the fashion, and
so berattle the common stages—so they call them—
that many wearing rapiers are afraid of goose quills
and dare scarce come thither.
HAMLET: What, are they children? Who maintains 'em?   345
How are they escoted? Will they pursue the quality no
longer than they can sing? Will they not say after-
wards, if they should grow themselves to common

117

players—as it is most like, if their means are no better—their writers do them wrong to make them ex-   350
claim against their own succession?

ROSENCRANTZ: Faith, there has been much to-do on
both sides, and the nation holds it no sin to tar them
to controversy. There was for a while no money bid
for argument unless the poet and the player went to   355
cuffs in the question.

HAMLET: Is 't possible?

GUILDENSTERN: O, there has been much throwing about of brains.

HAMLET: Do the boys carry it away?   360

ROSENCRANTZ: Ay, that they do, my lord—Hercules
and his load too.

HAMLET: It is not very strange; for my uncle is King of
Denmark, and those that would make mouths at him
while my father lived give twenty, forty, fifty, a   365
hundred ducats apiece for his picture in little. 'Sblood
there is something in this more than natural, if philosophy could find it out.

A flourish [of trumpets within].

GUILDENSTERN: There are the players.

HAMLET: Gentlemen, you are welcome to Elsinore. Your   370
hands, come then. Th' appurtenance of welcome is
fashion and ceremony. Let me comply with you in this
garb, lest my extent to the players, which, I tell you,
must show fairly outwards, should more appear like
entertainment than yours. You are welcome. But my   375
uncle-father and aunt-mother are deceived.

GUILDENSTERN: In what, my dear lord?

HAMLET: I am but mad north-north-west. When the
wind is southerly I know a hawk from a handsaw.

Enter Polonius.

POLONIUS: Well be with you, gentlemen!   380

HAMLET: Hark you, Guildenstern, and you too; at each
ear a hearer. That great baby you see there is not yet
out of his swaddling clouts.

ROSENCRANTZ: Haply he is the second time come to
them, for they say an old man is twice a child.   385

HAMLET: I will prophesy he comes to tell me of the players; mark it.—You say right, sir, o' Monday morning,
'twas then indeed.

POLONIUS: My lord, I have news to tell you.

HAMLET: My lord, I have news to tell you. When Ros-   390
cius was an actor in Rome—

118

POLONIUS: The actors are come hither, my lord.
HAMLET: Buzz, buzz!
POLONIUS: Upon my honor—
HAMLET: Then came each actor on his ass.
POLONIUS: The best actors in the world, either for   395
    tragedy, comedy, history, pastoral, pastoral-comical,
    historical-pastoral, tragical-historical, tragical-comical-
    historical-pastoral, scene individable, or poem unlim-
    ited. Seneca cannot be too heavy, nor Plautus too light.   400
    For the law of writ and the liberty, these are the only
    men.
HAMLET: O Jephthah, judge of Israel, what a treasure
    hadst thou!
POLONIUS: What a treasure had he, my lord?   405
HAMLET: Why,

"One fair daughter, and no more,
The which he lovèd passing well."

POLONIUS: [*Aside*] Still on my daughter.
HAMLET: Am I not i' the right, old Jephthah?   410
POLONIUS: If you call me Jephthah, my lord, I have a
    daughter that I love passing well.
HAMLET: Nay, that follows not.
POLONIUS: What follows then, my lord?
HAMLET: Why,   415

"As by lot, God wot,"

and then, you know,

"It came to pass, as most like it was"—

the first row of the pious chanson will show you more,
for look where my abridgement comes.   420

Enter the Players.

You are welcome, masters; welcome, all. I am glad to
see thee well. Welcome, good friends. O, old friend!
Why, thy face is valanced since I saw thee last. Com'st
thou to beard me in Denmark? What, my young lady
and mistress! By 'r Lady, your ladyship is nearer to   425
heaven than when I saw you last, by the altitude of a
chopine. Pray God your voice, like a piece of uncur-
rent gold, be not cracked within the ring. Masters, you
are all welcome. We'll e'en to 't like French falconers,
fly at anything we see. We'll have a speech straight.   430

119

Come, give us a taste of your quality. Come, a passionate speech.

FIRST PLAYER: What speech, my good lord?

HAMLET: I heard thee speak me a speech once, but it
was never acted, or if it was, not above once, for the 435
play, I remember, pleased not the million; 'twas cav-
iar to the general. But it was—as I received it, and
others, who judgments in such matters cried in the
top of mine—an excellent play, well digested in the
scenes, set down with as much modesty as cunning. I 440
remember one said there were no sallets in the lines to
make the matter savory, nor no matter in the phrase
that might indict the author of affectation, but called it
an honest method, as wholesome as sweet, and by
very much more handsome than fine. One speech in 't 445
I chiefly loved: 'twas Aeneas' tale to Dido, and there-
about of it especially when he speaks of Priam's
slaughter. If it live in your memory, begin at this line:
let me see, let me see—

"The rugged Pyrrhus, like th' Hyrcanian beast"— 450

'Tis not so. It begins with Pyrrhus:

"The rugged Pyrrhus, he whose sable arms,
Black as his purpose, did the night resemble
When he lay couchèd in the ominous horse,
Hath now this dread and black complexion smeared 455
With heraldry more dismal. Head to foot
Now is he total gules, horridly tricked
With blood of fathers, mothers, daughters, sons,
Baked and impasted with the parching streets,
That lend a tyrannous and a damnèd light 460
To their lord's murder. Roasted in wrath and fire,
And thus o'ersizèd with coagulate gore,
With eyes like carbuncles, the hellish Pyrrhus
Old grandsire Priam seeks."

So proceed you. 465

POLONIUS: 'Fore God, my lord, well spoken, with good
accent and good discretion.

FIRST PLAYER: "Anon he finds him
Striking too short at Greeks. His antique sword,
Rebellious to his arm, likes where it falls, 470
Repugnant to command. Unequal matched,
Pyrrhus at Priam drives, in rage strikes wide,

120

But with the whiff and wind of his fell sword
Th' unnervèd father falls. Then senseless Ilium,
Seeming to feel this blow, with flaming top   475
Stoops to his base, and with a hideous crash
Takes prisoner Pyrrhus' ear. For, lo! His sword,
Which was declining on the milky head
Of reverend Priam, seeméd i' th' air to stick.
So as a painted tyrant Pyrrhus stood,   480
And, like a neutral to his will and matter,
Did nothing.
But as we often see against some storm
A silence in the heavens, the rack stand still,
The bold winds speechless, and the orb below   485
As hush as death, anon the dreadful thunder
Doth rend the region, so, after Pyrrhus' pause,
Arousèd vengeance sets him new a-work,
And never did the Cyclops' hammers fall
On Mars's armor forged for proof eterne   490
With less remorse than Pyrrhus' bleeding sword
Now falls on Priam.
Out, out, thou strumpet Fortune! All you gods
In general synod take away her power!
Break all the spokes and fellies from her wheel,   495
And bowl the round nave down the hill of heaven
As low as to the fiends!"
POLONIUS: This is too long.
HAMLET: It shall to the barber's with your beard.—Prithee,
say on. He's for a jig or a tale of bawdry, or he   500
sleeps. Say on; come to Hecuba.
FIRST PLAYER: "But who, ah woe! had seen the moblèd queen"—
HAMLET: "The moblèd queen"?
POLONIUS: That's good. "Moblèd queen" is good.
FIRST PLAYER: "Run barefoot up and down, threat'ning the flames   505
With bisson rheum, a clout upon that head
Where late the diadem stood, and, for a robe,
About her lank and all o'erteemèd loins
A blanket, in the alarm of fear caught up—
Who this had seen, with tongue in venom steeped,   510
'Gainst Fortune's state would treason have
pronounced.
But if the gods themselves did see her then
When she saw Pyrrhus make malicious sport
In mincing with his sword her husband's limbs,
The instant burst of clamor that she made,   515
Unless things mortal move them not at all,
Would have made milch the burning eyes of heaven,
And passion in the gods."

POLONIUS: Look whe'er he has not turned his color and
    has tears in 's eyes. Prithee, no more.   520
HAMLET: 'Tis well. I'll have thee speak out the rest of
    this soon.—Good my lord, will you see the players well
    bestowed? Do you hear, let them be well used, for they
    are the abstract and brief chronicles of the time. After
    your death you were better have a bad epitaph than   525
    their ill report while you live.
POLONIUS: My lord, I will use them according to their
    desert.
HAMLET: God's bodikin, man, much better. Use every
    man after his desert, and who shall scape whipping?   530
    Use them after your own honor and dignity. The less
    they deserve, the more merit is in your bounty. Take
    them in.
POLONIUS: Come, sirs.
HAMLET: Follow him, friends. We'll hear a play tomor-   535
    row. [*As they start to leave, Hamlet detains the First*
    Player.] Dost thou hear me, old friend? Can you play
    The Murder of Gonzago?
FIRST PLAYER: Ay, my lord.
HAMLET: We'll ha 't tomorrow night. You could, for   540
    a need, study a speech of some dozen or sixteen lines
    which I would set down and insert in 't, could you
    not?
FIRST PLAYER: Ay, my lord.
HAMLET: Very well. Follow that lord, and look you mock   545
    him not. (*Exeunt Polonius and Players.*) My good friends,
    I'll leave you till night. You are welcome to Elsinore.
ROSENCRANTZ: Good my lord!

                Exeunt Rosencrantz and Guildenstern.

HAMLET: Ay, so goodbye to you.—Now I am alone.
    O, what a rogue and peasant slave am I!   550
    Is it not monstrous that this player here,
    But in a fiction, in a dream of passion,
    Could force his soul so to his own conceit
    That from her working all his visage wanned,
    Tears in his eyes, distraction in his aspect,   555
    A broken voice, and his whole function suiting
    With forms to his conceit? And all for nothing!
    For Hecuba!
    What's Hecuba to him, or he to Hecuba,
    That he should weep for her? What would he do   560
    Had he the motive and the cue for passion
    That I have? He would drown the stage with tears
    And cleave the general ear with horrid speech,

Make mad the guilty and appall the free,
Confound the ignorant, and amaze indeed   565
The very faculties of eyes and ears. Yet I,
A dull and muddy-mettled rascal, peak
Like John-a-dreams, unpregnant of my cause,
And can say nothing—no, not for a king
Upon whose property and most dear life   570
A damned defeat was made. Am I a coward?
Who calls me villain? Breaks my pate across?
Plucks off my beard and blows it in my face?
Tweaks me by the nose? Gives me the lie i' the throat
As deep as to the lungs? Who does me this?   575
Ha, 'swounds, I should take it; for it cannot be
But I am pigeon-livered and lack gall
To make oppression bitter, or ere this
I should ha' fatted all the region kites
With this slave's offal. Bloody, bawdy villain!   580
Remorseless, treacherous, lecherous, kindless villain!
O, vengeance!
Why, what an ass am I! This is most brave,
That I, the son of a dear father murdered,
Prompted to my revenge by heaven and hell,   585
Must like a whore unpack my heart with words
And fall a-cursing, like a very drab,
A scullion! Fie upon 't, foh! About, my brain!
Hum, I have heard
That guilty creatures sitting at a play   590
Have by the very cunning of the scene
Been struck so to the soul that presently
They have proclaimed their malefactions;
For murder, though it have no tongue, will speak
With most miraculous organ. I'll have these players   595
Play something like the murder of my father
Before mine uncle. I'll observe his looks;
I'll tent him to the quick. If 'a do blench,
I know my course. The spirit that I have seen
May be the devil, and the devil hath power   600
T' assume a pleasing shape; yea, and perhaps,
Out of my weakness and my melancholy,
As he is very potent with such spirits,
Abuses me to damn me. I'll have grounds
More relative than this. The play's the thing   605
Wherein I'll catch the conscience of the King.

Exit.

123

ACT III

Scene I

Enter King, Queen, Polonius, Ophelia, Rosencrantz, Guildenstern, lords.

KING: And can you by no drift of conference
    Get from him why he puts on this confusion,
    Grating so harshly all his days of quiet
    With turbulent and dangerous lunacy?
ROSENCRANTZ: He does confess he feels himself distracted,   5
    But from what cause 'a will by no means speak.
GUILDENSTERN: Nor do we find him forward to be sounded,
    But with a crafty madness keeps aloof
    When we would bring him on to some confession
    Of his true state.
QUEEN: Did he receive you well?   10
ROSENCRANTZ: Most like a gentleman.
GUILDENSTERN: But with much forcing of his disposition.
ROSENCRANTZ: Niggard of question, but of our demands
    Most free in his reply.
QUEEN: Did you assay him
    To any pastime?   15
ROSENCRANTZ: Madam, it so fell out that certain players
    We o'erraught on the way. Of these we told him,
    And there did seem in him a kind of joy
    To hear of it. They are here about the court,
    And, as I think, they have already order   20
    This night to play before him.
POLONIUS: 'Tis most true,
    And he beseeched me to entreat Your Majesties
    To hear and see the matter.
KING: With all my heart, and it doth much content me
    To hear him so inclined.   25
    Good gentlemen, give him a further edge
    And drive his purpose into these delights.
ROSENCRANTZ: We shall, my lord.

                                  Exeunt Rosencrantz and Guildenstern.

KING: Sweet Gertrude, leave us too,
    For we have closely sent for Hamlet hither,
    That he, as 'twere by accident, may here   30
    Affront Ophelia.
    Her father and myself, lawful espials,
    Will so bestow ourselves that seeing, unseen,
    We may of their encounter frankly judge,
    And gather by him, as he is behaved,   35

If 't be th' affliction of his love or no
That thus he suffers for.
QUEEN: I shall obey you.
And for your part, Ophelia, I do wish
That your good beauties be the happy cause
Of Hamlet's wildness. So shall I hope your virtues   40
Will bring him to his wonted way again,
To both your honors.
OPHELIA: Madam, I wish it may.

Exit Queen.

POLONIUS: Ophelia, walk you here.—Gracious, so please you,
We will bestow ourselves. [*To Ophelia.*] Read on this
book,

[*Giving her a book*]

That show of such an exercise may color   45
Your loneliness. We are oft to blame in this—
'Tis too much proved—that with devotion's visage
And pious action we do sugar o'er
The devil himself.
KING: [*Aside*] O, 'tis too true!   50
How smart a lash that speech doth give my conscience!
The harlot's cheek, beautied with plastering art,
Is not more ugly to the thing that helps it
Than is my deed to my most painted word.
O heavy burden!   55
POLONIUS: I hear him coming. Let's withdraw, my lord.

The King and Polonius withdraw.

Enter Hamlet. [*Ophelia pretends to read a book.*]

HAMLET: To be, or not to be, that is the question:
Whether 'tis nobler in the mind to suffer
The slings and arrows of outrageous fortune,
Or to take arms against a sea of troubles   60
And by opposing end them. To die, to sleep—
No more—and by a sleep to say we end
The heartache and the thousand natural shocks
That flesh is heir to. 'Tis a consummation
Devoutly to be wished. To die, to sleep;   65
To sleep, perchance to dream. Ay, there's the rub,
For in that sleep of death what dreams may come,
When we have shuffled off this mortal coil,
Must give us pause. There's the respect

That makes calamity of so long life.   70
For who would bear the whips and scorns of time,
Th' oppressor's wrong, the proud man's contumely,
The pangs of disprized love, the law's delay,
The insolence of office, and the spurns
That patient merit of th' unworthy takes,   75
When he himself might his quietus make
With a bare bodkin? Who would fardels bear,
To grunt and sweat under a weary life,
But that the dread of something after death,
The undiscovered country from whose bourn   80
No traveler returns, puzzles the will,
And makes us rather bear those ills we have
Than fly to others that we know not of?
Thus conscience does make cowards of us all;
And thus the native hue of resolution   85
Is sicklied o'er with the pale cast of thought,
And enterprises of great pitch and moment
With this regard their currents turn awry
And lose the name of action.—Soft you now,
The fair Ophelia. Nymph, in thy orisons   90
Be all my sins remembered.
OPHELIA: Good my lord.
     How does your honor for this many a day?
HAMLET: I humbly thank you; well, well, well.
OPHELIA: My lord, I have remembrances of yours,
     That I have longèd long to redeliver.   95
     I pray you, now receive them.

                                                      [*She offers tokens.*]

HAMLET: No, not I. I never gave you aught.
OPHELIA: My honored lord, you know right well you did,
     And with them words of so sweet breath composed
     As made the things more rich. Their perfume lost,   100
     Take these again, for to the noble mind
     Rich gifts wax poor when givers prove unkind.
     There, my lord.

                                                      [*She gives tokens.*]

HAMLET: Ha, ha! Are you honest?
OPHELIA: My lord?   105
HAMLET: Are you fair?
OPHELIA: What means your lordship?
HAMLET: That if you be honest and fair, your honesty
     should admit no discourse to your beauty.

OPHELIA: Could beauty, my lord, have better commerce   110
    than with honesty?
HAMLET: Ay, truly, for the power of beauty will sooner
    transform honesty from what it is to a bawd than the
    force of honesty can translate beauty into his likeness.
    This was sometime a paradox, but now the time gives   115
    it proof. I did love you once.
OPHELIA: Indeed, my lord, you made me believe so.
HAMLET: You should not have believed me, for virtue
    cannot so inoculate our old stock but we shall relish of
    it. I loved you not.   120
OPHELIA: I was the more deceived.
HAMLET: Get thee to a nunnery. Why wouldst thou be a
    breeder of sinners? I am myself indifferent honest, but
    yet I could accuse me of such things that it were better
    my mother had not borne me: I am very proud, re-   125
    vengeful, ambitious, with more offenses at my beck
    than I have thoughts to put them in, imagination to
    give them shape, or time to act them in. What should
    such fellows as I do crawling between earth and
    heaven? We are arrant knaves all; believe none of us.   130
    Go thy ways to a nunnery. Where's your father?
OPHELIA: At home, my lord.
HAMLET: Let the doors be shut upon him, that he may
    play the fool nowhere but in 's own house. Farewell.
OPHELIA: O, help him, you sweet heavens!   135
HAMLET: If thou dost marry, I'll give thee this plague for
    thy dowry: be thou as chaste as ice, as pure as snow,
    thou shalt not escape calumny. Get thee to a nunnery,
    farewell. Or, if thou wilt needs marry, marry a fool,
    for wise men know well enough what monsters you   140
    make of them. To a nunnery, go, and quickly too. Fare-
    well.
OPHELIA: Heavenly powers, restore him!
HAMLET: I have heard of your paintings too, well
    enough. God hath given you one face, and you make   145
    yourselves another. You jig, you amble, and you
    lisp, you nickname God's creatures, and make your
    wantonness your ignorance. Go to, I'll no more on 't;
    it hath made me mad. I say we will have no more
    marriage. Those that are married already—all but   150
    one—shall live. The rest shall keep as they are. To a
    nunnery, go.

Exit.

OPHELIA: O, what a noble mind is here o'erthrown!
    The courtier's, soldier's, scholar's, eye, tongue, sword,

Th' expectancy and rose of the fair state,   155
The glass of fashion and the mold of form,
Th' observed of all observers, quite, quite down!
And I, of ladies most deject and wretched,
That sucked the honey of his music vows,
Now see that noble and most sovereign reason   160
Like sweet bells jangled out of tune and harsh,
That unmatched form and feature of blown youth
Blasted with ecstasy. O, woe is me,
T' have seen what I have seen, see what I see!

Enter King and Polonius.

KING: Love? His affections do not that way tend;   165
    Nor what he spake, though it lacked form a little,
    Was not like madness. There's something in his soul
    O'er which his melancholy sits on brood,
    And I do doubt the hatch and the disclose
    Will be some danger; which for to prevent,   170
    I have in quick determination
    Thus set it down: he shall with speed to England
    For the demand of our neglected tribute.
    Haply the seas and countries different
    With variable objects shall expel   175
    This something settled matter in his heart,
    Whereon his brains still beating puts him thus
    From fashion of himself. What think you on 't ?
POLONIUS: It shall do well. But yet do I believe
    The origin and commencement of his grief   180
    Spring from neglected love.—How now, Ophelia?
    You need not tell us what Lord Hamlet said;
    We heard it all.—My lord, do as you please,
    But, if you hold it fit, after the play
    Let his queen-mother all alone entreat him   185
    To show his grief. Let her be round with him;
    And I'll be placed, so please you, in the ear
    Of all their conference. If she finds him not,
    To England send him, or confine him where
    Your wisdom best shall think.   190
KING: It shall be so.
    Madness in great ones must not unwatched go.

                                                        Exeunt.

ACT III. SCENE II

Enter Hamlet and three of the Players.

HAMLET: Speak the speech, I pray you, as I pronounced
it to you, trippingly on the tongue. But if you mouth
it, as many of our players do, I had as lief the town
crier spoke my lines. Nor do not saw the air too much
with your hand, thus, but use all gently; for in the very   5
torrent, tempest, and, as I may say, whirlwind of your
passion, you must acquire and beget a temperance
that may give it smoothness. O, it offends me to the
soul to hear a robustious periwig-pated fellow tear a
passion to tatters, to very rags, to split the ears of the   10
groundlings, who for the most part are capable of
nothing but inexplicable dumb shows and noise. I
would have such a fellow whipped for o'erdoing Ter-
magant. It out-Herods Herod. Pray you, avoid it.
FIRST PLAYER: I warrant your honor.   15
HAMLET: Be not too tame neither, but let your own discretion be your tutor. Suit the action to the word, the
word to the action, with this special observance, that
you o'erstep not the modesty of nature. For anything
so o'erdone is from the purpose of playing, whose   20
end, both at the first and now, was and is to hold as
'twere the mirror up to nature, to show virtue her
feature, scorn her own image, and the very age and
body of the time his form and pressure. Now this
overdone or come tardy off, though it makes the un-   25
skillful laugh, cannot but make the judicious grieve,
the censure of the which one must in your allowance
o'erweigh a whole theater of others. O, there by players that I have not seen play, and heard others praise, and
that highly, not to speak it profanely, that, neither   30
having th' accent of Christians nor the gait of Christian, pagan, nor man, have so strutted and bellowed
that I have thought some of nature's journeymen had
made men and not made them well, they imitated humanity so abominably.   35
FIRST PLAYER: I hope we have reformed that indifferently
with us, sir.
HAMLET: O, reform it altogether. And let those that play
your clowns speak no more than is set down for them;
for there be of them that will themselves laugh, to set   40
on some quantity of barren spectators to laugh too,
though in the meantime some necessary question of
the play be then to be considered. That's villainous,

129

and shows a most pitiful ambition in the fool that uses
it. Go make you ready.   45

Exeunt Players.

Enter Polonius, Guildenstern, and Rosencrantz.

How now, my lord, will the King hear this piece of
work?
POLONIUS: And the Queen too, and that presently.
HAMLET: Bid the players make haste.

Exit Polonius.

Will you two help to hasten them?   50
ROSENCRANTZ: Ay, my lord.

Exeunt they two.

HAMLET: What ho, Horatio!

Enter Horatio.

HORATIO: Here, sweet lord, at your service.
HAMLET: Horatio, thou art e'en as just a man
    As e'er my conversation coped withal.
HORATIO: O, my dear lord—
HAMLET: Nay, do not think I flatter,   55
    For what advancement may I hope from thee
    That no revenue hast but thy good spirits
    To feed and clothe thee? Why should the poor be
        flattered?
    No, let the candied tongue lick absurd pomp,
    And crook the pregnant hinges of the knee   60
    Where thrift may follow fawning. Dost thou hear?
    Since my dear soul was mistress of her choice
    And could of men distinguish her election,
    Sh' hath sealed thee for herself, for thou hast been
    As one, in suffering all, that suffers nothing,   65
    A man that Fortune's buffets and rewards
    Hast ta'en with equal thanks; and blest are those
    Whose blood and judgment are so well commeddled
    That they are not a pipe for Fortune's finger
    To sound what stop she please. Give me that man   70
    That is not passion's slave, and I will wear him
    In my heart's core, ay, in my heart of heart,
    As I do thee.—Something too much of this.—

There is a play tonight before the King.
Once scene of it comes near the circumstance   75
Which I have told thee of my father's death.
I prithee, when thou seest that act afoot,
Even with the very comment of thy soul
Observe my uncle. If his occulted guilt
Do not itself unkennel in one speech,   .   80
It is a damnèd ghost that we have seen,
And my imaginations are as foul
As Vulcan's stithy. Give him heedful note,
For I mine eyes will rivet to his face,
And after we will both our judgments join   85
In censure of his seeming.
HORATIO: Well, my lord.
If 'a steal aught the whilst this play is playing
And scape detecting, I will pay the theft.

[*Flourish*]. *Enter trumpets and kettledrums, King, Queen, Polonius, Ophelia,*
[*Rosencrantz, Guildenstern, and other lords, with guards carrying torches.*]

HAMLET: They are coming to the play. I must be idle.
Get you a place.   90

[*The King, Queen, and courtiers sit.*]

KING: How fares our cousin Hamlet?
HAMLET: Excellent, i' faith, of the chameleon's dish: I eat the air, promise-
crammed. You cannot feed capons so.
KING: I have nothing with this answer, Hamlet. These
words are not mine.   95
HAMLET: No, nor mine now. [*To Polonius.*] My lord,
you played once i' th' university, you say?
POLONIUS: That did I, my lord, and was accounted a
good actor.
HAMLET: What did you enact?   100
POLONIUS: I did enact Julius Caesar. I was killed i' the
Capitol; Brutus killed me.
HAMLET: It was a brute part of him to kill so capital a calf there.—Be
the players ready?
ROSENCRANTZ: Ay, my lord. They stay upon your pa-   105
tience.
QUEEN: Come hither, my dear Hamlet, sit by me.
HAMLET: No, good Mother, here's metal more attractive.
POLONIUS: [*To the King*] Oho, do you mark that?
HAMLET: Lady, shall I lie in your lap?   110

[*Lying down at Ophelia's feet.*]

131

OPHELIA: No, my lord.

HAMLET: I mean, my head upon your lap?

OPHELIA: Ay, my lord.

HAMLET: Do you think I meant country matters?

OPHELIA: I think nothing, my lord. 115

HAMLET: That's a fair thought to lie between maids'
legs.

OPHELIA: What is, my lord?

HAMLET: Nothing.

OPHELIA: You are merry, my lord. 120

HAMLET: Who, I?

OPHELIA: Ay, my lord.

HAMLET: O God, your only jig maker. What should a
man do but be merry? For look you how cheerfully my
mother looks, and my father died within 's two hours. 125

OPHELIA: Nay, 'tis twice two months, my lord.

HAMLET: So long? Nay then, let the devil wear black, for
I'll have a suit of sables. O heavens! Die two months
ago, and not forgotten yet? Then there's hope a great
man's memory may outlive his life half a year. But, 130
by 'r Lady, 'a must build churches, then, or else shall
'a suffer not thinking on, with the hobbyhorse, whose
epitaph is "For O, for O, the hobbyhorse is forgot."

The trumpets sound. Dumb show follows.

*Enter a King and a Queen [very lovingly]; the Queen embracing him, and he her.
[She kneels, and makes show of protestation unto him.] He takes her up, and
declines his head upon her neck. He lies him down upon a bank of flowers. She,
seeing him asleep, leaves him. Anon comes in another man, takes off his crown,
kisses it, pours poison in the sleeper's ears, and leaves him. The Queen returns,
finds the King dead, makes passionate action. The Poisoner with some three or
four come in again, seem to condole with her. The dead body is carried away. The
Poisoner woos the Queen with gifts; she seems harsh awhile, but in the end
accepts love.*

Exeunt players.

OPHELIA: What means this, my lord?

HAMLET: Marry, this' miching mallico; it means mis- 135
chief.

OPHELIA: Belike this show imports the argument of the
play.

Enter Prologue.

HAMLET: We shall know by this fellow. The players cannot keep counsel; they'll tell all. 140

OPHELIA: Will 'a tell us what this show meant?
HAMLET: Ay, or any show that you will show him. Be
   not you ashamed to show, he'll not shame to tell you
   what it means.
OPHELIA: You are naught, you are naught. I'll mark the   145
   play.
PROLOGUE: For us, and for our tragedy,
   Here stooping to your clemency,
   We beg you hearing patiently.

                                                           Exit.

HAMLET: Is this a prologue, or the posy of a ring?   150
OPHELIA: 'Tis brief, my lord.
HAMLET: As woman's love.

Enter [two Players as] King and Queen.

PLAYER KING: Full thirty times hath Phoebus' cart gone round
   Neptune's salt wash and Tellus' orbèd ground,
   And thirty dozen moons with borrowed sheen   155
   About the world have times twelve thirties been,
   Since love our hearts and Hymen did our hands
   Unite commutual in most sacred bands.
PLAYER QUEEN: So many journeys may the sun and moon
   Make us again count o'er ere love be done!   160
   But, woe is me, you are so sick of late,
   So far from cheer and from your former state,
   That I distrust you. Yet, though I distrust,
   Discomfort you, my lord, it nothing must.
   For women's fear and love hold quantity;   165
   In neither aught, or in extremity.
   Now, what my love is, proof hath made you know,
   And as my love is sized, my fear is so.
   Where love is great, the little doubts are fear;
   Where little fears grow great, great love grows there. 170
PLAYER KING: Faith, I must leave thee, love, and shortly too;
   My operant powers their functions leave to do.
   And thou shalt live in this fair world behind,
   Honored, beloved; and haply one as kind
   For husband shalt thou—
PLAYER QUEEN: O, confound the rest!   175
   Such love must needs be treason in my breast.
   In second husband let me be accurst!
   None wed the second but who killed the first.
HAMLET: Wormwood, wormwood.
PLAYER QUEEN: The instances that second marriage move   180
   Are base respects of thrift, but none of love.

A second time I kill my husband dead
When second husband kisses me in bed.
PLAYER KING: I do believe you think what now you speak,
But what we do determine oft we break. 185
Purpose is but the slave to memory,
Of violent birth, but poor validity,
Which now, like fruit unripe, sticks on the tree,
But fall unshaken when they mellow be.
Most necessary 'tis that we forget 190
To pay ourselves what to ourselves is debt.
What to ourselves in passion we propose,
The passion ending, doth the purpose lose.
The violence of either grief or joy
Their own enactures with themselves destroy. 195
Where joy most revels, grief doth most lament;
Grief joys, joy grieves, on slender accident.
This world is not for aye, nor 'tis not strange
That even our loves should with our fortunes change;
For 'tis a question left us yet to prove, 200
Whether love lead fortune, or else fortune love.
The great man down, you mark his favorite flies;
The poor advanced makes friends of enemies.
And hitherto doth love on fortune tend;
For who not needs shall never lack a friend, 205
And who in want a hollow friend doth try
Directly seasons him his enemy.
But, orderly to end where I begun,
Our wills and fates do so contrary run
That our devices still are overthrown; 210
Our thoughts are ours, their ends none of our own.
So think thou wilt no second husband wed,
But die thy thoughts when thy first lord is dead.
PLAYER QUEEN: Nor earth to me give food, nor heaven light,
Sport and repose lock from me day and night, 215
To desperation turn my trust and hope,
An anchor's cheer in prison be my scope!
Each opposite that blanks the face of joy
Meet what I would have well and it destroy!
Both here and hence pursue me lasting strife 220
If, once a widow, ever I be a wife!
HAMLET: If she should break it now!
PLAYER KING: 'Tis deeply sworn. Sweet, leave me here awhile;
My spirits grow dull, and fain I would beguile
The tedious day with sleep.
PLAYER QUEEN: Sleep rock thy brain, 225
And never come mischance between us twain!

[He sleeps.] Exit Player Queen.

134

HAMLET: Madam, how like you this play?

QUEEN: The lady doth protest too much, methinks.

HAMLET: O, but she'll keep her word.

KING: Have you heard the argument? Is there no offense   230
 in 't?

HAMLET: No, no, they do but jest, poison in jest. No offense i' the world.

KING: What do you call the play?

HAMLET: *The Mousetrap.* Marry, how? Tropically.   235
 This play is the image of a murder done in Vienna.
 Gonzago is the Duke's name, his wife, Baptista. You
 shall see anon. 'Tis a knavish piece of work, but what
 of that? Your Majesty, and we that have free souls, it
 touches us not. Let the galled jade wince, our withers   240
 are unwrung.

Enter Lucianus.

 This is one Lucianus, nephew to the King.

OPHELIA: You are as good as a chorus, my lord.

HAMLET: I could interpret between you and your love,
 if I could see the puppets dallying.   245

OPHELIA: You are keen, my lord, you are keen.

HAMLET: It would cost you a groaning to take off mine
 edge.

OPHELIA: Still better, and worse.

HAMLET: So you mis-take your husbands.—Begin, mur-   250
 derer; leave thy damnable faces and begin. Come, the
 croaking raven doth bellow for revenge.

LUCIANUS: Thoughts black, hands apt, drugs fit, and time agreeing,
 Confederate season, else no creature seeing,
 Thou mixture rank, of midnight weeds collected,   255
 With Hecate's ban thrice blasted, thrice infected,
 Thy natural magic and dire property
 On wholesome life usurp immediately.

 [He pours the poison into the sleeper's ear.]

HAMLET: 'A poisons him i' the garden for his estate. His
 name's Gonzago. The story is extant, and written in   260
 very choice Italian. You shall see anon how the murderer gets the love of Gonzago's wife.

 [Claudius rises.]

OPHELIA: The King rises.

HAMLET: What, frighted with false fire?

QUEEN: How fares my lord?   265
POLONIUS: Give o'er the play.
KING: Give me some light. Away!
POLONIUS: Lights, lights, lights!

Exeunt all but Hamlet and Horatio.

HAMLET: "Why, let the strucken deer go weep,
     The hart ungallèd play.   270
  For some must watch, while some must sleep;
     Thus runs the world away."
 Would not this, sir, and a forest of feathers—if the rest
of my fortunes turn Turk with me—with two Provin-
cial roses on my razed shoes, get me a fellowship in a   275
cry of players?
HORATIO: Half a share.
HAMLET: A whole one, I.
   "For thou dost know, O Damon dear,
     This realm dismantled was   280
   Of Jove himself, and now reigns here
     A very, very—pajock."
HORATIO: You might have rhymed.
HAMLET: O good Horatio, I'll take the ghost's word for
a thousand pound. Didst perceive?   285
HORATIO: Very well, my lord.
HAMLET: Upon the talk of the poisoning?
HORATIO: I did very well note him.

Enter Rosencrantz and Guildenstern.

HAMLET: Aha! Come, some music! Come, the record-
ers.   290

   "For if the King like not the comedy,
   Why then, belike, he likes it not, perdy."

 Come, some music.
GUILDENSTERN: Good my lord, vouchsafe me a word
with you.   295
HAMLET: Sir, a whole history.
GUILDENSTERN: The King, sir—
HAMLET: Ay, sir, what of him?
GUILDENSTERN: Is in his retirement marvelous dis-
tempered.   300
HAMLET: With drink, sir?
GUILDENSTERN: No, my lord, with choler.
HAMLET: Your wisdom should show itself more richer
to signify this to the doctor, for for me to put him to

his purgation would perhaps plunge him into more 305
choler.

GUILDENSTERN: Good my lord, put your discourse into
some frame and start not so wildly from my affair.

HAMLET: I am tame, sir. Pronounce.

GUILDENSTERN: The Queen, your mother, in most great 310
affliction of spirit, hath sent me to you.

HAMLET: You are welcome.

GUILDENSTERN: Nay, good my lord, this courtesy is not
of the right breed. If it shall please you to make me a
wholesome answer, I will do your mother's command- 315
ment; if not, your pardon and my return shall be the
end of my business.

HAMLET: Sir, I cannot.

ROSENCRANTZ: What, my lord?

HAMLET: Make you a wholesome answer; my wit's dis- 320
eased. But, sir, such answer as I can make, you shall
command, or rather, as you say, my mother. Therefore
no more, but to the matter. My mother, you say—

ROSENCRANTZ: Then thus she says: your behavior hath
struck her into amazement and admiration. 325

HAMLET: O wonderful son, that can so stonish a mother!
But is there no sequel at the heels of this mother's admiration? Impart.

ROSENCRANTZ: She desires to speak with you in her
closet ere you go to bed. 330

HAMLET: We shall obey, were she ten times our mother.
Have you any further trade with us?

ROSENCRANTZ: My lord, you once did love me.

HAMLET: And do still, by these pickers and stealers.

ROSENCRANTZ: Good my lord, what is your cause of dis- 335
temper? You do surely bar the door upon your own
liberty if you deny your griefs to your friend.

HAMLET: Sir, I lack advancement.

ROSENCRANTZ: How can that be, when you have the
voice of the King himself for your succession in Den- 340
mark?

HAMLET: Ay, sir, but "While the grass grows"—the
proverb is something musty.

Enter the Players with recorders.

O, the recorders. Let me see one.

[*He takes a recorder.*]

To withdraw with you: why do you go about to recover 345
the wind of me, as if you would drive me into a toil?

137

GUILDENSTERN: O, my lord, if my duty be too bold, my
    love is too unmannerly.
HAMLET: I do not well understand that. Will you play
    upon this pipe? 350
GUILDENSTERN: My lord, I cannot.
HAMLET: I pray you.
GUILDENSTERN: Believe me, I cannot.
HAMLET: I do beseech you.
GUILDENSTERN: I know no touch of it, my lord. 355
HAMLET: It is as easy as lying. Govern these ventages
    with your fingers and thumb, give it breath with your
    mouth, and it will discourse most eloquent music.
    Look you, these are the stops.
GUILDENSTERN: But these cannot I command to any 360
    utterance of harmony. I have not the skill.
HAMLET: Why, look you now, how unworthy a thing
    you make of me! You would play upon me, you would
    seem to know my stops, you would pluck out the heart
    of my mystery, you would sound me from my lowest 365
    note to the top of my compass, and there is much
    music, excellent voice, in this little organ, yet cannot
    you make it speak. 'Sblood, do you think I am easier
    to be played on than a pipe? Call me what instrument
    you will, though you can fret me, you cannot play 370
    upon me.

Enter Polonius.

    God bless you, sir!
POLONIUS: My lord, the Queen would speak with you,
    and presently.
HAMLET: Do you see yonder cloud that's almost in 375
    shape of a camel?
POLONIUS: By the Mass and 'tis, like a camel indeed.
HAMLET: Methinks it is like a weasel.
POLONIUS: It is backed like a weasel.
HAMLET: Or like a whale? 380
POLONIUS: Very like a whale.
HAMLET: Then I will come to my mother by and by.
    [*Aside.*] They fool me to the top of my bent.—I will
    come by and by.
POLONIUS: I will say so. 385

Exit.

HAMLET: "By and by" is easily said. Leave me, friends.

Exeunt all but Hamlet.

'Tis now the very witching time of night,
When churchyards yawn and hell itself breathes out
Contagion to this world. Now could I drink hot blood
And do such bitter business as the day   390
Would quake to look on. Soft, now to my mother.
O heart, lose not thy nature! Let not ever
The soul of Nero enter this firm bosom.
Let me be cruel, not unnatural;
I will speak daggers to her, but use none.   395
My tongue and soul in this be hypocrites:
How in my words soever she be shent,
To give them seals never my soul consent!

Exit.

ACT III. SCENE III

Enter King, Rosencrantz, and Guildenstern.

KING: I like him not, nor stands it safe with us
    To let his madness range. Therefore prepare you.
    I your commission will forthwith dispatch,
    And he to England shall along with you.
    The terms of our estate may not endure   5
    Hazard so near 's as doth hourly grow
    Out of his brows.
GUILDENSTERN: We will ourselves provide.
    Most holy and religious fear it is
    To keep those many many bodies safe
    That live and feed upon Your Majesty.   10
ROSENCRANTZ: The single and peculiar life is bound
    With all the strength and armor of the mind
    To keep itself from noyance, but much more
    That spirit upon whose weal depends and rests
    The lives of many. The cess of majesty   15
    Dies not alone, but like a gulf doth draw
    What's near it with it; or it is a massy wheel
    Fixed on the summit of the highest mount,
    To whose huge spokes ten thousand lesser things
    Are mortised and adjoined, which, when it falls,   20
    Each small annexment, petty consequence,
    Attends the boisterous ruin. Never alone
    Did the King sigh, but with a general groan.
KING: Arm you, I pray you, to this speedy voyage,
    For we will fetters put about this fear,   25
    Which now goes too free-footed.
ROSENCRANTZ: We will haste us.

Exeunt Gentlemen [Rosencrantz and Guildenstern].

139

Enter Polonius.

POLONIUS: My lord, he's going to his mother's closet.
Behind the arras I'll convey myself
To hear the process. I'll warrant she'll tax him home,
And, as you said—and wisely was it said—   30
'Tis meet that some more audience than a mother,
Since nature makes them partial, should o'erhear
The speech, of vantage. Fare you well, my liege.
I'll call upon you ere you go to bed
And tell you what I know.
KING: Thanks, dear my lord.   35

Exit Polonius.

O, my offense is rank, it smells to heaven;
It hath the primal eldest curse upon 't,
A brother's murder. Pray can I not,
Though inclination be as sharp as will;
My stronger guilt defeats my strong intent,   40
And like a man to double business bound
I stand in pause where I shall first begin,
And both neglect. What if this cursèd hand,
Were thicker than itself with brother's blood,
Is there not rain enough in the sweet heavens   45
To wash it white as snow? Whereto serves mercy
But to confront the visage of offense?
And what's in prayer but this twofold force,
To be forestallèd ere we come to fall,
Or pardoned being down? Then I'll look up.   50
My fault is past. But, O, what form of prayer
Can serve my turn? "Forgive me my foul murder"?
That cannot be, since I am still possessed
Of those effects for which I did the murder:
My crown, mine own ambition, and my queen.   55
May one be pardoned and retain th' offense?
In the corrupted currents of this world
Offense's gilded hand may shove by justice,
And oft 'tis seen the wicked prize itself
Buys out the law. But 'tis not so above.   60
There is no shuffling, there the action lies
In his true nature, and we ourselves compelled,
Even to the teeth and forehead of our faults,
To give in evidence. What then? What rests?
Try what repentance can. What can it not?   65
Yet what can it, when one cannot repent?
O wretched state! O bosom black as death!

140

O limèd soul, that, struggling to be free,
Art more engaged! Help, angels! Make assay.
Bow, stubborn knees, and heart with strings of steel,   70
Be soft as sinews of the newborn babe!
All may be well.

                                                      [*He kneels.*]

Enter Hamlet.

HAMLET: Now might I do it pat, now 'a is a-praying;
And now I'll do it. [*He draws his sword.*] And so 'a goes to heaven.
And so am I revenged. That would be scanned: 75
A villain kills my father, and for that,
I, his sole son, do this same villain send
To heaven.
Why, this is hire and salary, not revenge.
'A took my father grossly, full of bread,   80
With all his crimes broad blown, as flush as May;
And how his audit stands who knows save heaven?
But in our circumstance and course of thought
'Tis heavy with him. And am I then revenged,
To take him in the purging of his soul,   85
When he is fit and seasoned for his passage?
No!
Up, sword, and know thou a more horrid hent.

                                             [*He puts up his sword.*]

When he is drunk asleep, or in his rage,
Or in th' incestuous pleasure of his bed,   90
At game a-swearing, or about some act
That has no relish of salvation in 't—
Then trip him, that his heels may kick at heaven,
And that his soul may be as damned and black
As hell, whereto it goes. My mother stays.   95
This physic but prolongs thy sickly days.

                                                      Exit.

KING: My words fly up, my thoughts remain below.
Words without thoughts never to heaven go.

                                                      Exit.

Act III. Scene IV

Enter [Queen] Gertrude and Polonius.

POLONIUS: 'A will come straight. Look you lay home to him.
    Tell him his pranks have been too broad to bear with,
    And that Your Grace hath screened and stood between
    Much heat and him. I'll shroud me even here.
    Pray you, be round with him.   5
HAMLET: *(Within)* Mother, Mother, Mother!
QUEEN: I'll warrant you, fear me not.
    Withdraw, I hear him coming.

                          [Polonius hides behind the arras.]

Enter Hamlet.

HAMLET: Now, Mother, what's the matter?
QUEEN: Hamlet, thou hast thy father much offended.   10
HAMLET: Mother, you have my father much offended.
QUEEN: Come, come, you answer with an idle tongue.
HAMLET: Go, go, you question with a wicked tongue.
QUEEN: Why, how now, Hamlet?
HAMLET: What's the matter now?
QUEEN: Have your forgot me?
HAMLET: No, by the rood, not so: 15
    You are the Queen, your husband's brother's wife,
    And—would it were not so!—you are my mother.
QUEEN: Nay, then, I'll set those to you that can speak.
HAMLET: Come, come, and sit you down; you shall not budge.
    You go not till I set you up a glass   20
    Where you may see the inmost part of you.
QUEEN: What wilt thou do? Thou wilt not murder me?
    Help, ho?
POLONIUS: *[Behind the arras]* What ho! Help!
HAMLET: *[Drawing]* How now? A rat? Dead for a ducat, dead!   25

                     [He thrusts his rapier through the arras.]

POLONIUS: *[Behind the arras]* O, I am slain!

                             [He falls and dies.]

QUEEN: O me, what hast thou done?
HAMLET: Nay, I know not. Is it the King?
QUEEN: O, what a rash and bloody deed is this!
HAMLET: A bloody deed—almost as bad, good Mother,
    As kill a king and marry with his brother.   30

QUEEN: As kill a king!
HAMLET: Ay, lady, it was my word.

[*He parts the arras and discovers Polonius.*]

Thou wretched, rash, introducing fool, farewell!
I took thee for thy better. Take thy fortune.
Thou find'st to be too busy is some danger.—
Leave wringing of your hands. Peace, sit you down,   35
And let me wring your heart, for so I shall,
If it be made of penetrable stuff,
If damnèd custom have not brazed it so
That it be proof and bulwark against sense.
QUEEN: What have I done, that thou dar'st wag thy tongue   40
In noise so rude against me?
HAMLET: Such an act
That blurs the grace and blush of modesty,
Calls virtue hypocrite, takes off the rose
From the fair forehead of an innocent love
And sets a blister there, makes marriage vows   45
As false as dicers' oaths. O, such a deed
As from the body of contraction plucks
The very soul, and sweet religion makes
A rhapsody of words. Heaven's face does glow
O'er this solidity and compound mass   50
With tristful visage, as against the doom,
Is thought-sick at the act.
QUEEN: Ay me, what act,
That roars so loud and thunders in the index?
HAMLET: [*Showing her two likenesses*]
Look here upon this picture, and on this,
The counterfeit presentment of two brothers.   55
See what a grace was seated on this brow:
Hyperion's curls, the front of Jove himself,
An eye like Mars to threaten and command,
A station like the herald Mercury
New-lighted on a heaven-kissing hill—   60
A combination and a form indeed
Where every god did seem to set his seal
To give the world assurance of a man.
This was your husband. Look you now what follows:
Here is your husband, like a mildewed ear,   65
Blasting his wholesome brother. Have you eyes?
Could you on this fair mountain leave to feed
And batten on this moor? Ha, have you eyes?
You cannot call it love, for at your age
The heyday in the blood is tame, it's humble,   70
And waits upon the judgment, and what judgment

Would step from this to this? Sense, sure, you have,
Else could you not have motion, but sure that sense
Is apoplexed, for madness would not err,
Nor sense to ecstasy was ne'er so thralled,   75
But it reserved some quantity of choice
To serve in such a difference. What devil was 't
That thus hath cozened you at hoodman-blind?
Eyes without feeling, feeling without sight,
Ears without hands or eyes, smelling sans all,   80
Or but a sickly part of one true sense
Could not so mope. O shame, where is thy blush?
Rebellious hell,
If thou canst mutine in a matron's bones,
To flaming youth let virtue be as wax   85
And melt in her own fire. Proclaim no shame
When the compulsive ardor gives the charge,
Since frost itself as actively doth burn,
And reason panders will.
QUEEN: O Hamlet, speak no more!   90
　　Thou turn'st my eyes into my very soul,
　　And there I see such black and grainèd spots
　　As will not leave their tinct.
HAMLET: Nay, but to live
　　In the rank sweat of an enseamèd bed,
　　Stewed in corruption, honeying and making love   95
　　Over the nasty sty!
QUEEN: O, speak to me no more!
　　These words like daggers enter in my ears.
　　No more, sweet Hamlet!
HAMLET: A murderer and a villain,
　　A slave that is not twentieth part the tithe   100
　　Of your precedent lord, a vice of kings,
　　A cutpurse of the empire and the rule,
　　That from a shelf the precious diadem stole
　　And put it in his pocket!
QUEEN: No more!   105

Enter Ghost [in his nightgown].

HAMLET: A king of shreds and patches—
　　Save me, and hover o'er me with your wings,
　　You heavenly guards! What would your gracious figure?
QUEEN: Alas, he's mad!
HAMLET: Do you not come your tardy son to chide,   110
　　That, lapsed in time and passion, lets go by
　　Th' important acting of your dread command?
　　O, say!

GHOST: Do not forget. This visitation
Is but to whet thy almost blunted purpose.   115
But look, amazement on thy mother sits.
O, step between her and her fighting soul!
Conceit in weakest bodies strongest works.
Speak to her, Hamlet.
HAMLET: How is it with you, lady?
QUEEN: Alas, how is 't with you,   120
That you do bend your eye on vacancy,
And with th' incorporal air do hold discourse?
Forth at your eyes your spirits wildly peep,
And, as the sleeping soldiers in th' alarm,
Your bedded hair, like life in excrements,   125
Start up and stand on end. O gentle son,
Upon the heat and flame of thy distemper
Sprinkle cool patience. Whereon do you look?
HAMLET: On him, on him! Look you how pale he glares!
His form and cause conjoined, preaching to stones,   130
Would make them capable.—Do not look upon me,
Lest with this piteous action you convert
My stern effects. Then what I have to do
Will want true color—tears perchance for blood.
QUEEN: To whom do you speak this?   135
HAMLET: Do you see nothing there?
QUEEN: Nothing at all, yet all that is I see.
HAMLET: Nor did you nothing hear?
QUEEN: No, nothing but ourselves.
HAMLET: Why, look you there, look how it steals away!   140
My father, in his habit as he lived!
Look where he goes even now out at the portal!

                                                        Exit Ghost.

QUEEN: This is the very coinage of your brain.
This bodiless creation ecstasy
Is very cunning in.   145
HAMLET: Ecstasy?
My pulse as yours doth temperately keep time,
And makes as healthful music. It is not madness
That I have uttered. Bring me to the test,
And I the matter will reword, which madness   150
Would gambol from. Mother, for love of grace,
Lay not that flattering unction to your soul
That not your trespass but my madness speaks.
It will but skin and film the ulcerous place,
Whiles rank corruption, mining all within,   155
Infects unseen. Confess yourself to heaven,

Repent what's past, avoid what is to come,
And do not spread the compost on the weeds
To make them ranker. Forgive me this my virtue;
For in the fatness of these pursy times   160
Virtue itself of vice must pardon beg,
Yea, curb and woo for leave to do him good.
QUEEN: O Hamlet, thou hast cleft my heart in twain.
HAMLET: O, throw away the worser part of it,
And live the purer with the other half.   165
Good night. But go not to my uncle's bed;
Assume a virtue, if you have it not.
That monster, custom, who all sense doth eat,
Of habits devil, is angel yet in this,
That to the use of actions fair and good   170
He likewise gives a frock or livery
That aptly is put on. Refrain tonight,
And that shall lend a kind of easiness
To the next abstinence; the next more easy;
For use almost can change the stamp of nature,   175
And either . . . the devil, or throw him out
With wondrous potency. Once more, good night;
And when you are desirous to be blest,
I'll blessing beg of you. For this same lord,

[*Pointing to Polonius*]   180

I do repent; but heaven hath pleased it so
To punish me with this, and this with me,
That I must be their scourge and minister.
I will bestow him, and will answer well
The death I gave him. So, again, good night.
I must be cruel only to be kind.   185
This bad begins, and worse remains behind.
One word more, good lady.
QUEEN: What shall I do?
HAMLET: Not this by no means that I bid you do:
Let the bloat king tempt you again to bed,
Pinch wanton on your cheek, call you his mouse,   190
And let him, for a pair of reechy kisses,
Or paddling in your neck with his damned fingers,
Make you to ravel all this matter out
That I essentially am not in madness,
But mad in craft. 'Twere good you let him know,   195
For who that's but a queen, fair, sober, wise,
Would from a paddock, from a bat, a gib,
Such dear concernings hide? Who would do so?
No, in despite of sense and secrecy,
Unpeg the basket on the house's top,   200
Let the birds fly, and like the famous ape,

To try conclusions, in the basket creep
And break your own neck down.
QUEEN: Be thou assured, if words be made of breath,
And breath of life, I have no life to breathe   205
What thou hast said to me.
HAMLET: I must to England. You know that?
QUEEN: Alack,
I had forgot. 'Tis so concluded on.
HAMLET: There's letters sealed, and my two schoolfellows,
Whom I will trust as I will adders fanged,   210
They bear the mandate; they must sweep my way
And marshal me to knavery. Let it work.
For 'tis the sport to have the enginer
Hoist with his own petard, and 't shall go hard
But I will delve one yard below their mines   215
And blow them at the moon. O, 'tis most sweet
When in one line two crafts directly meet.
This man shall set me packing.
I'll lug the guts into the neighbor room.
Mother, good night indeed. This counselor   220
Is now most still, most secret, and most grave,
Who was in life a foolish prating knave.—
Come, sir, to draw toward an end with you.—
Good night, Mother.

> *Exeunt [separately, Hamlet dragging in Polonius].*

ACT IV

SCENE I

Enter King and Queen, with Rosencrantz and Guildenstern.

KING: There's matter in these sighs, these profound heaves.
You must translate; 'tis fit we understand them.
Where is your son?
QUEEN: Bestow this place on us a little while.

> *Exeunt Rosencrantz and Guildenstern.*

Ah, mine own lord, what have I seen tonight!   5
KING: What, Gertrude? How does Hamlet?
QUEEN: Mad as the sea and wind when both contend
Which is the mightier. In his lawless fit,
Behind the arras hearing something stir,
Whips out his rapier, cries, "A rat, a rat!"   10
And in this brainish apprehension kills
The unseen good old man.

147

KING: O heavy deed!
  It had been so with us, had we been there.
  His liberty is full of threats to all—
  To you yourself, to us, to everyone.   15
  Alas, how shall this bloody deed be answered?
  It will be laid to us, whose providence
  Should have kept short, restrained, and out of haunt
  This mad young man. But so much was our love,
  We would not understand what was most fit,   20
  But, like the owner of a foul disease,
  To keep it from divulging, let it feed
  Even on the pith of life. Where is he gone?
QUEEN: To draw apart the body he hath killed,
  O'er whom his very madness, like some ore   25
  Among a mineral of metals base,
  Shows itself pure: 'a weeps for what is done.
KING: O Gertrude, come away!
  The sun no sooner shall the mountains touch
  But we will ship him hence, and this vile deed   30
  We must with all our majesty and skill
  Both countenance and excuse.—Ho, Guildenstern!

Enter Rosencrantz and Guildenstern.

  Friends both, go join you with some further aid.
  Hamlet in madness hath Polonius slain,
  And from his mother's closet hath he dragged him.   35
  Go seek him out, speak fair, and bring the body
  Into the chapel. I pray you, haste in this.

                              Exeunt Rosencrantz and Guildenstern.

  Come, Gertrude, we'll call up our wisest friends
  And let them know both what we mean to do
  And what's untimely done.   40
  Whose whisper o'er the world's diameter,
  As level as the cannon to his blank,
  Transports his poisoned shot, may miss our name
  And hit the woundless air. O, come away!
  My soul is full of discord and dismay.   45

                                             Exeunt.

ACT IV. SCENE II

Enter Hamlet.

HAMLET: Safely stowed.
ROSENCRANTZ, GUILDENSTERN: (*Within*): Hamlet! Lord
  Hamlet!

HAMLET: But soft, what noise? Who calls on Hamlet? O,
    here they come.   5

Enter Rosencrantz and Guildenstern.

ROSENCRANTZ: What have you done, my lord, with the dead body?
HAMLET: Compounded it with dust, whereto 'tis kin.
ROSENCRANTZ: Tell us where 'tis, that we may take it thence
    And bear it to the chapel.
HAMLET: Do not believe it.
ROSENCRANTZ: Believe what?   10
HAMLET: That I can keep your counsel and not mine
    own. Besides, to be demanded of a sponge, what rep-
    lication should be made by the son of a king?
ROSENCRANTZ: Take you me for a sponge, my lord?   15
HAMLET: Ay sir, that soaks up the King's countenance,
    his rewards, his authorities. But such officers do the
    King best service in the end. He keeps them, like an
    ape, in the corner of his jaw, first mouthed to be last
    swallowed. When he needs what you have gleaned, it   20
    is but squeezing you, and, sponge, you shall be dry
    again.
ROSENCRANTZ: I understand you not, my lord.
HAMLET: I am glad of it. A knavish speech sleeps in a
    foolish ear.   25
ROSENCRANTZ: My lord, you must tell us where the
    body is and go with us to the King.
HAMLET: The body is with the King, but the King is not
    with the body. The King is a thing—
GUILDENSTERN: A thing, my lord?   30
HAMLET: Of nothing. Bring me to him. Hide fox, and all after!

                                                           Exeunt.

ACT IV. SCENE III

Enter King, and two or three.

KING: I have sent to seek him, and to find the body.
    How dangerous is it that this man goes loose!
    Yet must not we put the strong law on him.
    He's loved of the distracted multitude,
    Who like not in their judgment, but their eyes,   5
    And where 'tis so, th' offender's scourge is weighed,
    But never the offense. To bear all smooth and even,
    This sudden sending him away must seem
    Deliberate pause. Diseases desperate grown
    By desperate appliance are relieved,   10
    Or not at all.

Enter Rosencrantz, [Guildenstern,] and all the rest.

How now, what hath befall'n?
ROSENCRANTZ: Where the dead body is bestowed, my lord,
    We cannot get from him.
KING: But where is he?
ROSENCRANTZ: Without, my lord; guarded, to know your pleasure.
KING: Bring him before us.
ROSENCRANTZ: Ho! Bring in the lord.   15

They enter [with Hamlet].

KING: Now, Hamlet, where's Polonius?
HAMLET: At supper.
KING: At supper? Where?
HAMLET: Not where he eats, but where 'a is eaten. A
    certain convocation of politic worms are e'en at him.   20
    Your worm is your only emperor for diet. We fat all
    creatures else to fat us, and we fat ourselves for mag-
    gots. Your fat king and your lean beggar is but
    variable service—two dishes, but to one table. That's
    the end.   25
KING: Alas, alas!
HAMLET: A man may fish with the worm that hath eat
    of a king, and eat of the fish that hath fed of that
    worm.
KING: What dost thou mean by this?   30
HAMLET: Nothing but to show you how a king may go
    a progress through the guts of a beggar.
KING: Where is Polonius?
HAMLET: In heaven. Send thither to see. If your messen-
    ger find him not there, seek him i' th' other place your-   35
    self. But if indeed you find him not within this month,
    you shall nose him as you go up the stairs into the
    lobby.
KING: [*To some attendants*] Go seek him there.
HAMLET: 'A will stay till you come.   40

                                          Exeunt attendants.

KING: Hamlet, this deed, for thine especial safety—
    Which we do tender, as we dearly grieve
    For that which thou hast done—must send thee hence
    With fiery quickness. Therefore prepare thyself.
    The bark is ready, and the wind at help,   45
    Th' associates tend, and everything is bent
    For England.
HAMLET: For England!

KING: Ay, Hamlet.

HAMLET: Good. 50

KING: So is it, if thou knew'st our purposes.

KING: I see a cherub that sees them. But come, for
England! Farewell, dear Mother.

KING: Thy loving father, Hamlet.

HAMLET: My mother. Father and mother is man and 55
wife, man and wife is one flesh, and so, my mother.
Come, for England!

KING: Follow him at foot; tempt him with speed aboard.
Delay it not. I'll have him hence tonight.
Away! For everything is sealed and done 60
That else leans on th' affair. Pray you, make haste.

Exeunt all but the King.

And, England, if my love thou hold'st at aught—
As my great power thereof may give thee sense,
Since yet thy cicatrice looks raw and red
After the Danish sword, and thy free awe 65
Pays homage to us—thou mayst not coldly set
Our sovereign process, which imports at full,
By letters congruing to that effect,
The present death of Hamlet. Do it, England,
For like the hectic in my blood he rages, 70
And thou must cure me. Till I know 'tis done,
Howe'er my haps, my joys were ne'er begun.

Exit.

ACT IV. SCENE IV

Enter Fortinbras with his army over the stage.

FORTINBRAS: Go, Captain, from me greet the Danish king.
Tell him that by his license Fortinbras
Craves the conveyance of a promised march
Over his kingdom. You know the rendezvous.
If that His Majesty would aught with us, 5
We shall express our duty in his eye;
And let him know so.

CAPTAIN: I will do 't, my lord.

FORTINBRAS: Go softly on.

Exeunt all but the Captain.

Enter Hamlet, Rosencrantz, [Guildenstern,] etc.

HAMLET: Good sir, whose powers are these? 10

CAPTAIN: They are of Norway, sir.

151

HAMLET: How purposed, sir, I pray you?
CAPTAIN: Against some part of Poland.
HAMLET: Who commands them, sir?
CAPTAIN: The nephew to old Norway, Fortinbras.   15
HAMLET: Goes it against the main of Poland, sir,
    Or for some frontier?
CAPTAIN: Truly to speak, and with no addition,
    We go to gain a little patch of ground
    That hath in it no profit but the name.   20
    To pay five ducats, five, I would not farm it;
    Nor will it yield to Norway or the Pole
    A ranker rate, should it be sold in fee.
HAMLET: Why, then the Polack never will defend it.
CAPTAIN: Yes, it is already garrisoned.   25
HAMLET: Two thousand souls and twenty thousand ducats
    Will not debate the question of this straw.
    This is th' impostume of much wealth and peace,
    That inward breaks, and shows no cause without
    Why the man dies. I humbly thank you, sir.   30
CAPTAIN: God b' wi' you, sir.

                                                          Exit.

ROSENCRANTZ: Will 't please you go, my lord?
HAMLET: I'll be with you straight. Go a little before.

                                        Exeunt all except Hamlet.

    How all occasions do inform against me
    And spur my dull revenge! What is a man,
    If his chief good and market of his time   35
    Be but to sleep and feed? A beast, no more.
    Sure he that made us with such large discourse,
    Looking before and after, gave us not
    That capability and godlike reason
    To fust in us unused. Now, whether it be   40
    Bestial oblivion, or some craven scruple
    Of thinking too precisely on th' event—
    A thought which, quartered, hath but one part wisdom
    And ever three parts coward—I do not know
    Why yet I live to say "This thing's to do,"   45
    Sith I have cause, and will, and strength, and means
    To do 't. Examples gross as earth exhort me:
    Witness this army of such mass and charge,
    Led by a delicate and tender prince,
    Whose spirit with divine ambition puffed   50
    Makes mouths at the invisible event,
    Exposing what is mortal and unsure

To all that fortune, death, and danger dare,
Even for an eggshell. Rightly to be great
Is not to stir without great argument,   55
But greatly to find quarrel in a straw
When honor's at the stake. How stand I then,
That have a father killed, a mother stained,
Excitements of my reason and my blood,
And let all sleep, while to my shame I see   60
The imminent death of twenty thousand men
That for a fantasy and trick of fame
Go to their graves like beds, fight for a plot
Whereon the numbers cannot try the cause,
Which is not tomb enough and continent   65
To hide the slain? O, from this time forth
My thoughts be bloody or be nothing worth!

Exit.

ACT IV. SCENE V

Enter Horatio, [Queen] Gertrude, and a Gentleman.

QUEEN: I will not speak with her.
GENTLEMAN: She is importunate,
    Indeed distract. Her mood will needs be pitied.
QUEEN: What would she have?
GENTLEMAN: She speaks much of her father, says she hears
    There's tricks i' the world, and hems, and beats her heart,   5
    Spurns enviously at straws, speaks things in doubt
    That carry but half sense. Her speech is nothing,
    Yet the unshapèd use of it doth move
    The hearers to collection; they yawn at it,
    And botch the words up fit to their own thoughts,   10
    Which, as her winks and nods and gestures yield them,
    Indeed would make one think there might be thought,
    Though nothing sure, yet much unhappily.
HORATIO: 'Twere good she were spoken with, for she may strew
    Dangerous conjectures in ill-breeding minds.   15
QUEEN: Let her come in.

Exit Gentleman.

    [*Aside.*] To my sick soul, as sin's true nature is,
    Each toy seems prologue to some great amiss.
    So full of artless jealousy is guilt,
    It spills itself in fearing to be spilt.   20

Enter Ophelia [distracted].

153

OPHELIA: Where is the beauteous majesty of Denmark?
QUEEN: How now, Ophelia?
OPHELIA: (*She sings*)

> "How should I your true love know
> From another one?
> By his cockle hat and staff,   25
> And his sandal shoon."

QUEEN: Alas, sweet lady, what imports this song?
OPHELIA: Say you? Nay, pray you, mark.

(Song).

> "He is dead and gone, lady,
> He is dead and gone;   30
> At his head as grass-green turf,
> At his heels a stone."

   Oho!
QUEEN: Nay, but Ophelia—
OPHELIA: Pray you, mark.   35
[*Sings.*] "White his shroud as the mountain snow"—

Enter King.

QUEEN: Alas, look here, my lord.
OPHELIA: "Larded with sweet flowers;

(Song.)

> Which bewept to the ground did not go
> With true-love showers."   40

KING: How do you, pretty lady?
OPHELIA: Well, God 'ild you! They say the owl was a
   baker's daughter. Lord, we know what we are, but
   know not what we may be. God be at your table!
KING: Conceit upon her father.   45
OPHELIA: Pray let's have no words of this; but when
   they ask you what it means, say you this:

(Song.)

> "Tomorrow is Saint Valentine's day,
> All in the morning betime,
> And I a maid at your window,   50
> To be your Valentine.

154

Then up he rose, and donned his clothes,
And dupped the chamber door,
Let in the maid, that out a maid
Never departed more." 55

KING: Pretty Ophelia—
OPHELIA: Indeed, la, without an oath, I'll make an end
on 't:
[Sings.]"By Gis and by Saint Charity,
Alack, and fie for shame! 60
Young men will do 't, if they come to 't;
By Cock, they are to blame.
Quoth she, 'Before you tumbled me,
You promised me to wed.'"
He answers: 65
"'So would I ha' done, by yonder sun,
An thou hadst not come to my bed.'"
KING: How long hath she been thus?
OPHELIA: I hope all will be well. We must be patient,
but I cannot choose but weep to think they would lay 70
him i' the cold ground. My brother shall know of it.
And so I thank you for your good counsel. Come, my
coach! Good night, ladies, good night, sweet ladies,
good night, good night.

Exit.

KING: [To Horatio]
Follow her close. Give her good watch, I pray you. 75

Exit Horatio.

O, this is the poison of deep grief; it springs
All from her father's death—and now behold!
O Gertrude, Gertrude,
When sorrows come, they come not single spies,
But in battalions. First, her father slain; 80
Next, your son gone, and he most violent author
Of his own just remove; the people muddied,
Thick and unwholesome in their thoughts and whispers
For good Polonius' death—and we have done but greenly
In hugger-mugger to inter him; poor Ophelia 85
Divided from herself and her fair judgment,
Without the which we are pictures or mere beasts;
Last, and as much containing as all these,
Her brother is in secret come from France,
Feeds on his wonder, keeps himself in clouds, 90
And wants not buzzers to infect his ear

155

With pestilent speeches of his father's death,
Wherein necessity, of matter beggared,
Will nothing stick our person to arraign
In ear and ear. O my dear Gertrude, this,   95
Like to a murdering piece, in many places
Gives me superfluous death.

                                                    [*A noise within*].

QUEEN: Alack, what noise is this?
KING: Attend!
    Where are my Switzers? Let them guard the door.   100

Enter a Messenger.

    What is the matter?
MESSENGER: Save yourself, my lord!
    The ocean, overpeering of his list,
    Eats not the flats with more impetuous haste
    Than young Laertes, in a riotous head,
    O'erbears your officers. The rabble call him lord,   105
    And, as the world were now but to begin,
    Antiquity forgot, custom not known,
    The ratifiers and props of every word,
    They cry, "Choose we! Laertes shall be king!"
    Caps, hands, and tongues applaud it to the clouds,   110
    "Laertes shall be king, Laertes king!"

                                                    [*A noise within*].

QUEEN: How cheerfully on the false trail they cry!
    O, this is counter, you false Danish dogs!

Enter Laertes with others.

KING: The doors are broke.
LAERTES: Where is this King?—Sirs, stand you all without.   115
ALL: No, let's come in.
LAERTES: I pray you, give me leave.
ALL: We will, we will.
LAERTES: I thank you. Keep the door. [*Exeunt followers.*] O thou
        vile king,
    Give me my father!
QUEEN: [*Holding him*] Calmly, good Laertes.   120
LAERTES: That drop of blood that's calm proclaims me bastard,
    Cries cuckold to my father, brands the harlot
    Even here, between the chaste unsmirchèd brow
    Of my true mother.

KING: What is the cause, Laertes,
    That thy rebellion looks so giantlike?   125
    Let him go, Gertrude. Do not fear our person.
    There's such divinity doth hedge a king
    That treason can but peep to what it would,
    Acts little of his will. Tell me, Laertes,
    Why thou art thus incensed. Let him go, Gertrude.   130
    Speak, man.
LAERTES: Where is my father?
KING: Dead.
QUEEN: But not by him.
KING: Let him demand his fill.
LAERTES: How came he dead? I'll not be juggled with.
    To hell, allegiance! Vows, to the blackest devil!
    Conscience and grace, to the profoundest pit!   135
    I dare damnation. To this point I stand,
    That both the worlds I give to negligence,
    Let come what comes, only I'll be revenged
    Most throughly for my father.
KING: Who shall stay you?   140
LAERTES: My will, not all the world's.
    And for my means, I'll husband them so well
    They shall go far with little.
KING: Good Laertes,
    If you desire to know the certainty
    Of your dear father, is 't writ in your revenge   145
    That, swoopstake, you will draw both friend and foe,
    Winner and loser?
LAERTES: None but his enemies.
KING: Will you know them, then?
LAERTES: To his good friends thus wide I'll ope my arms,   150
    And like the kind life-rendering pelican
    Repast them with my blood.
KING: Why, now you speak
    Like a good child and a true gentleman.
    That I am guiltless of your father's death,
    And am most sensibly in grief for it,   155
    It shall as level to your judgment 'pear
    As day does to your eye.

                                  [A noise within].

LAERTES: How now, what noise is that?

Enter Ophelia.

KING: Let her come in.
LAERTES: O heat, dry up my brains! Tears seven times salt
    Burn out the sense and virtue of mine eye!   160

By heaven, thy madness shall be paid with weight
Till our scale turn the beam. O rose of May!
Dear maid, kind sister, sweet Ophelia!
O heavens, is 't possible a young maid's wits
Should be as mortal as an old man's life?   165
Nature is fine in love, and where 'tis fine
It sends some precious instance of itself
After the thing it loves.
OPHELIA:
         "They bore him barefaced on the bier,   *(Song.)*
         Hey non nonny, nonny, hey nonny,   170
         And in his grave rained many a tear—"

Fare you well, my dove!
LAERTES: Hadst thou thy wits and didst persuade revenge,
    It could not move thus.
OPHELIA: You must sing "A-down a-down," and you   175
    "call him a-down-a." O, how the wheel becomes it!
    It is the false steward that stole his master's daughter.
LAERTES: This nothing's more than matter.
OPHELIA: There's rosemary, that's for remembrance;
    pray you, love, remember. And there is pansies; that's   180
    for thoughts.
LAERTES: A document in madness, thoughts and remembrance fitted.
OPHELIA: There's fennel for you, and columbines.
    There's rue for you, and here's some for me; we may   185
    call it herb of grace o' Sundays. You must wear your
    rue with a difference. There's a daisy. I would give
    you some violets, but they withered all when my father
    died. They say 'a made a good end—
    [*Sings.*] "For bonny sweet Robin is all my joy."   190
LAERTES: Thought and affliction, passion, hell itself,
    She turns to favor and to prettiness.
OPHELIA: "And will 'a not come again?   *(Song.)*
         And will 'a not come again?
         No, no, he is dead.   195
         Go to thy deathbed,
         He never will come again.

         "His beard was as white as snow,
         All flaxen was his poll.
         He is gone, he is gone.   200
         And we cast away moan.
         God ha' mercy on his soul!"

And of all Christian souls, I pray God. God b' wi' you.

Exit.

LAERTES: Do you see this, O God?

KING: Laertes, I must commune with your grief,   205
    Or you deny me right. Go but apart,
    Make choice of whom your wisest friends you will,
    And they shall hear and judge twixt you and me.
    If by direct or by collateral hand
    They find us touched, we will our kingdom give,   210
    Our crown, our life, and all that we call ours
    To you in satisfaction; but if not,
    Be you content to lend your patience to us,
    And we shall jointly labor with your soul
    To give it due content.

LAERTES: Let this be so.   215
    His means of death, his obscure funeral—
    No trophy, sword, nor hatchment o'er his bones,
    No noble rite, nor formal ostentation—
    Cry to be heard, as 'twere from heaven to earth,
    That I must call 't in question.

KING: So you shall,   220
    And where th' offense is, let the great ax fall.
    I pray you, go with me.

Exeunt.

ACT IV. SCENE VI

Enter Horatio and others.

HORATIO: What are they that would speak with me?

GENTLEMAN: Seafaring men, sir. They say they have let-
    ters for you.

HORATIO: Let them come in.

Exit Gentleman.

    I do not know from what part of the world   5
    I should be greeted, if not from Lord Hamlet.

Enter Sailors.

FIRST SAILOR: God bless you, sir.

HORATIO: Let him bless thee too.

FIRST SAILOR: 'A shall, sir, an please him. There's a
    letter for you, sir—it came from th' ambassador that   10
    was bound for England—if your name be Horatio, as
    I am let to know it is.

[He gives a letter.]

HORATIO: [*Reads*] "Horatio, when thou shalt have overlooked this, give these fellows some means to the King;
they have letters for him. Ere we were two days old at   15
sea, a pirate of very warlike appointment gave us
chase. Finding ourselves too slow of sail, we put on a
compelled valor, and in the grapple I boarded them.
On the instant they got clear of our ship, so I alone
became their prisoner. They have dealt with me like   20
thieves of mercy, but they knew what they did: I am to
do a good turn for them. Let the King have the letters
I have sent, and repair thou to me with as much speed
as thou wouldest fly death. I have words to speak in
thine ear will make thee dumb, yet are they much too   25
light for the bore of the matter. These good fellows will
bring thee where I am. Rosencrantz and Guildenstern
hold their course for England. Of them I have much to
tell thee. Farewell.
He that knowest thine, Hamlet."   30
Come, I will give you way for these your letters,
And do 't the speedier that you may direct me
To him from whom you brought them.

Exeunt.

ACT IV. SCENE VII

Enter King and Laertes.

KING: Now must your conscience my acquittance seal,
And you must put me in your heart for friend,
Sith you have heard, and with a knowing ear,
That he which hath your noble father slain
Pursued my life.
LAERTES: It well appears. But tell me   5
Why you proceeded not against these feats
So crimeful and so capital in nature,
As by your safety, greatness, wisdom, all things else,
You mainly were stirred up.
KING: O, for two special reasons,   10
Which may to you perhaps seem much unsinewed,
But yet to me they're strong. The Queen his mother
Lives almost by his looks, and for myself—
My virtue or my plague, be it either which—
She is so conjunctive to my life and soul   15
That, as the star moves not but in his sphere,
I could not but by her. The other motive
Why to a public count I might not go
Is the great love the general gender bear him,

160

Who, dipping all his faults in their affection,   20
Work like the spring that turneth wood to stone,
Convert his gyves to graces, so that my arrows,
Too slightly timbered for so loud a wind,
Would have reverted to my bow again
But not where I had aimed them.   25
LAERTES: And so have I a noble father lost,
A sister driven into desperate terms,
Whose worth, if praises may go back again,
Stood challenger on mount of all the age
For her perfections. But my revenge will come.   30
KING: Break not your sleeps for that. You must not think
That we are made of stuff so flat and dull
That we can let our beard be shook with danger
And think it pastime. You shortly shall hear more.
I loved your father, and we love ourself;   35
And that, I hope, will teach you to imagine—

Enter a Messenger with letters.

How now? What news?
MESSENGER: Letters, my lord, from Hamlet:
This to Your Majesty, this to the Queen.

                                                    [He gives letters.]

KING: From Hamlet? Who brought them?
MESSENGER: Sailors, my lord, they say. I saw them not.   40
They were given me by Claudio. He received them
Of him that brought them.
KING: Laertes, you shall hear them.—
Leave us.

                                                    Exit Messenger.

[Reads.] "High and mighty, you shall know I am set
naked on your kingdom. Tomorrow shall I beg leave   45
to see your kingly eyes, when I shall, first asking your
pardon, thereunto recount the occasion of my sudden
and more strange return. Hamlet."
What should this mean? Are all the rest come back?
Or is it some abuse, and no such thing?   50
LAERTES: Know you the hand?
KING: 'Tis Hamlet's character. "Naked!"
And in a postscript here he says "alone."
Can you devise me?
LAERTES: I am lost in it, my lord. But let him come.
It warms the very sickness in my heart   55

161

That I shall live and tell him to his teeth,
"Thus dist thou."
KING: If it be so, Laertes—
     As how should it be so? How otherwise?—
     Will you be ruled by me?
LAERTES: Ay, my lord,
     So you will not o'errule me to a peace.   60
KING: To thine own peace. If he be now returned,
     As checking at his voyage, and that he means
     No more to undertake it, I will work him
     To an exploit, now ripe in my device,
     Under the which he shall not choose but fall;   65
     And for his death no wind of blame shall breathe,
     But even his mother, shall uncharge the practice
     And call it accident.
LAERTES: My lord, I will be ruled,
     The rather if you could devise it so
     That I might be the organ.
KING: It falls right.   70
     You have been talked of since your travel much,
     And that in Hamlet's hearing, for a quality
     Wherein they say you shine. Your sum of parts
     Did not together pluck such envy from him
     As did that one, and that, in my regard,   75
     Of the unworthiest siege.
LAERTES: What part is that, my lord?
KING: A very ribbon in the cap of youth,
     Yet needful too, for youth no less becomes
     The light and careless livery that it wears   80
     Than settled age his sables and his weeds
     Importing health and graveness. Two months since
     Here was a gentleman of Normandy.
     I have seen myself, and served against, the French,
     And they can well on horseback, but this gallant   85
     Had witchcraft in 't; he grew unto his seat,
     And to such wondrous doing brought his horse
     As had he been incorpsed and demi-natured
     With the brave beast. So far he topped my thought
     That I in forgery of shapes and tricks   90
     Come short of what he did.
LAERTES: A Norman was 't?
KING: A Norman.
LAERTES: Upon my life, Lamord.
KING: The very same.
LAERTES: I know him well. He is the brooch indeed
     And gem of all the nation.   95
KING: He made confession of you,
     And gave you such a masterly report

For art and exercise in your defense,
And for your rapier most especial,
That he cried out 'twould be a sight indeed   100
If one could match you. Th' escrimers of their nation,
He swore, had neither motion, guard, nor eye
If you opposed them. Sir, this report of his
Did Hamlet so envenom with his envy
That he could nothing do but wish and beg   105
Your sudden coming o'er, to play with you.
Now, out of this—
LAERTES: What out of this, my lord?
KING: Laertes, was your father dear to you?
Or are you like the painting of a sorrow,
A face without a heart?
LAERTES: Why ask you this?   110
KING: Not that I think you did not love your father,
But that I know love is begun by time,
And that I see, in passages of proof,
Time qualifies the spark and fire of it.
There lives within the very flame of love   115
A kind of wick or snuff that will abate it,
And nothing is at a like goodness still,
For goodness, growing to a pleurisy,
Dies in his own too much. That we would do,
We should do when we would; for this "would" changes   120
And hath abatements and delays as many
As there are tongues, are hands, are accidents,
And then this "should" is like a spendthrift sigh,
That hurts by easing. But, to the quick o' th' ulcer:
Hamlet comes back. What would you undertake   125
To show yourself in deed your father's son
More than in words?
LAERTES: To cut his throat i' the church.
KING: No place, indeed, should murder sanctuarize;
Revenge should have no bounds. But good Laertes,
Will you do this, keep close within your chamber.   130
Hamlet returned shall know you are come home.
We'll put on those shall praise your excellence
And set a double varnish on the fame
The Frenchman gave you, bring you in fine together,
And wager on your heads. He, being remiss,   135
Most generous, and free from all contriving,
Will not peruse the foils, so that with ease,
Or with a little shuffling, you may choose
A sword unbated, and in a pass of practice
Requite him for your father.   140
LAERTES: I will do 't,
And for that purpose I'll anoint my sword.

I bought an unction of a mountebank
So mortal that, but dip a knife in it,
Where it draws blood no cataplasm so rare,
Collected from all simples that have virtue   145
Under the moon, can save the thing from death
That is but scratched withal. I'll touch my point
With this contagion, that if I gall him slightly,
It may be death.
KING: Let's further thing of this,
     Weigh what convenience both of time and means   150
     May fit us to our shape. If this should fail,
     And that our drift look through our bad performance,
     'Twere better not assayed. Therefore this project
     Should have a back or second, that might hold
     If this did blast in proof. Soft, let me see.   155
     We'll make a solemn wager on your cunnings—
     I ha 't!
     When in your motion you are hot and dry—
     As make your bouts more violent to that end—
     And that he calls for drink, I'll have prepared him 160
     A chalice for the nonce, whereon but sipping,
     If he by chance escape your venomed stuck,
     Our purpose may hold there. [*A cry within.*] But stay,
         what noise?

Enter Queen.

QUEEN: One woe doth tread upon another's heel,
     So fast they follow. Your sister's drowned, Laertes.   165
LAERTES: Drowned! O, where?
QUEEN: There is a willow grows askant the brook,
     That shows his hoar leaves in the glassy stream;
     Therewith fantastic garlands did she make
     Of crowflowers, nettles, daisies, and long purples,   170
     That liberal shepherds give a grosser name,
     But our cold maids do dead men's fingers call them.
     There on the pendent boughs her crownet weeds
     Clamb'ring to hang, an envious sliver broke,
     When down her weedy trophies and herself   175
     Fell in the weeping brook. Her clothes spread wide,
     And mermaidlike awhile they bore her up,
     Which time she chanted snatches of old lauds,
     As one incapable of her own distress,
     Or like a creative native and endued   180
     Unto that element. But long it could not be
     Till that her garments, heavy with their drink,
     Pulled the poor wretch from her melodious lay
     To muddy death.

LAERTES: Alas, then she is drowned?
QUEEN: Drowned, drowned.   185
LAERTES: Too much of water hast thou, poor Ophelia,
   And therefore I forbid my tears. But yet
   It is our trick; nature her custom holds,
   Let shame say what it will. [*He weeps.*] When these are
   gone,
   The woman will be out. Adieu, my lord.   190
   I have a speech of fire that fain would blaze,
   But that this folly douts it.

                                                                        Exit.

KING: Let's follow, Gertrude.
   How much I had to do to calm his rage!
   Now fear I this will give it start again;
   Therefore let's follow.   195

                                                                       Exeunt.

ACT V

SCENE I

Enter two Clowns [with spades and mattocks].

FIRST CLOWN: Is she to be buried in Christian burial,
   when she willfully seeks her own salvation?
SECOND CLOWN: I tell thee she is; therefore make her
   grave straight. The crowner hath sat on her, and finds
   it Christian burial.   5
FIRST CLOWN: How can that be, unless she drowned her-
   self in her own defense?
SECOND CLOWN: Why, 'tis found so.
FIRST CLOWN: It must be *se offendendo*, it cannot be
   else. For here lies the point: if I drown myself wittingly,   10
   it argues an act, and an act hath three branches—it is
   to act, to do, and to perform. Argal, she drowned herself wittingly.
SECOND CLOWN: Nay, but hear you, goodman delver—
FIRST CLOWN: Give me leave. Here lies the water; good.   15
   Here stands the man; good. If the man go to this wa-
   ter and drown himself, it is, will he, nill he, he goes,
   mark you that. But if the water come to him and
   drown him, he drowns not himself. Argal, he that is
   not guilty of his own death shortens not his own life.   20
SECOND CLOWN: But is this law?
FIRST CLOWN: Ay, marry, is 't—crowner's quest law.

SECOND CLOWN: Will you ha' the truth on 't? If this had
not been a gentlewoman, she should have been bur-
ied out o' Christian burial.   25
FIRST CLOWN: Why, there thou sayst. And the more
pity that great folk should have countenance in this
world to drown or hang themselves more than their
even-Christian. Come, my spade. There is no ancient
gentlemen but gardeners, ditchers, and grave makers.   30
They hold up Adam's profession.
SECOND CLOWN: Was he a gentleman?
FIRST CLOWN: 'A was the first that ever bore arms.
SECOND CLOWN: Why, he had none.
FIRST CLOWN: What, art a heathen? How dost thou un-   35
derstand the Scripture? The Scripture says Adam
digged. Could he dig without arms? I'll put another
question to thee. If thou answerest me not to the purpose, confess thyself—
SECOND CLOWN: Go to.   40
FIRST CLOWN: What is he that builds stronger than ei-
ther the mason, the shipwright, or the carpenter?
SECOND CLOWN: The gallows maker, for that frame out-
lives a thousand tenants.
FIRST CLOWN: I like thy wit well, in good faith. The gal-   45
lows does well. But how does it well? It does well to
those that do ill. Now thou dost ill to say the gallows
is built stronger than the church. Argal, the gallows
may do well to thee. To 't again, come.
SECOND CLOWN: "Who builds stronger than a mason, a   50
shipwright, or a carpenter?"
FIRST CLOWN: Ay, tell me that, an unyoke.
SECOND CLOWN: Marry, now I can tell.
FIRST CLOWN: To 't.
SECOND CLOWN: Mass, I cannot tell.   55

Enter Hamlet and Horatio [at a distance].

FIRST CLOWN: Cudgel thy brains no more about it, for
your dull ass will not mend his pace with beating;
and when you are asked this question next, say "a
grave maker." The houses he makes lasts till dooms-
day. Go get thee in and fetch me a stoup of liquor.   60

Exit Second Clown. [First Clown digs.]

(Song.)

"In youth, when I did love, did love,
Methought it was very sweet,

To contract—O—the time for—a—my behove,
O, methought there—a—was nothing—a—meet."

HAMLET: Has this fellow no feeling of his business, 'a   65
  sings in grave-making?
HORATIO: Custom hath made it in him a property of
  easiness.
HAMLET: 'Tis e'en so. The hand of little employment
  hath the daintier sense.   70
FIRST CLOWN:

                                                    (Song.)

        "But age with his stealing steps
          Hath clawed me in his clutch,
        And hath shipped me into the land,
          As if I had never been such."

                                    [He throws up a skull.]

HAMLET: That skull had a tongue in it and could sing   75
  once. How the knave jowls it to the ground, as if
  'twere Cain's jawbone, that did the first murder! This
  might be the pate of a politician, which this ass now
  o'erreaches, one that would circumvent God, might
  it not?   80
HORATIO: It might, my lord.
HAMLET: Or of a courtier, which could say, "Good mor-
  row, sweet lord! How dost thou, sweet lord?" This
  might be my Lord Such-a-one, that praised my Lord
  Such-a-one's horse when 'a meant to beg it, might   85
  it not?
HORATIO: Ay, my lord.
HAMLET: Why, e'en so, and now my Lady Worm's,
  chapless, and knocked about the mazard with a sex-
  ton's spade. Here's fine revolution, an we had the trick   90
  to see 't. Did these bones cost no more the breeding
  but to play at loggets with them? Mine ache to think
  on 't.
FIRST CLOWN:

                                                    (Song.)

        "A pickax and a spade, a spade,
          For and a shrouding sheet;   95
        O, a pit of clay for to be made
          For such a guest is meet."

[He throws up another skull.]

HAMLET: There's another. Why may not that be the skull
of a lawyer? Where be his quiddities now, his quillities, his cases, his tenures, and his tricks? Why does   100
he suffer this mad knave now to knock him about the
sconce with a dirty shovel, and will not tell him of his
action of battery? Hum, this fellow might be in 's time
a great buyer of land, with his statutes, his recogni-
zances, his fines, his double vouchers, his recoveries.   105
Is this the fine of his fines and the recovery of his
recoveries, to have his fine pate full of fine dirt? Will
his vouchers vouch him no more of his purchases, and
double ones too, than the length and breadth of a
pair of indentures? The very conveyances of his lands   110
will scarcely lie in this box, and must th' inheritor
himself have no more, ha?
HORATIO: Not a jot more, my lord.
HAMLET: Is not parchment made of sheepskins?
HORATIO: Ay, my lord, and of calves' skins too.   115
HAMLET: They are sheep and calves which seek out assurance in that. I will speak to this fellow.—Whose
grave's this, sirrah?
FIRST CLOWN: Mine, sir.

[Sings.]

       "O, a pit of clay for to be made.   120
        For such a guest is meet."

HAMLET: I think it be thine, indeed, for thou liest in 't.
FIRST CLOWN: You lie out on 't, sir, and therefore 'tis not
yours: For my part, I do not lie in 't, yet it is mine.
HAMLET: Thou dost lie in 't, to be in 't and say it is   125
thine. 'Tis for the dead, not for the quick; therefore
thou liest.
FIRST CLOWN: 'Tis a quick lie, sir; 'twill away again from
me to you.
HAMLET: What man dost thou dig it for?   130
FIRST CLOWN: For no man, sir.
HAMLET: What woman, then?
FIRST CLOWN: For none, neither.
HAMLET: Who is to be buried in 't?
FIRST CLOWN: One that was a woman, sir, but, rest her   135
soul, she's dead.
HAMLET: How absolute the knave is! We must speak by
the card, or equivocation will undo us. By the Lord,

Horatio, this three years I have took note of it: the age
is grown so picked that the toe of the peasant comes so   140
near the heel of the courtier, he galls his kibe.—How
long hast thou been grave maker?
FIRST CLOWN: Of all the days i' the year, I came to 't that
day that our last king Hamlet overcame Fortinbras.
HAMLET: How long is that since?   145
FIRST CLOWN: Cannot you tell that? Every fool can tell
that. It was that very day that young Hamlet was
born—he that is mad and sent into England.
HAMLET: Ay, marry, why was he sent into England?
FIRST CLOWN: Why, because 'a was mad. 'A shall re-   150
cover his wits there, or if 'a do not, 'tis no great matter
there.
HAMLET: Why?
FIRST CLOWN: 'Twill not be seen in him there. There the
men are as mad as he.   155
HAMLET: How came he mad?
FIRST CLOWN: Very strangely, they say.
HAMLET: How strangely?
FIRST CLOWN: Faith, e'en with losing his wits.
HAMLET: Upon what ground?   160
FIRST CLOWN: Why, here in Denmark. I have been sex-
ton here, man and boy, thirty years.
HAMLET: How long will a man lie i' th' earth ere he rot?
FIRST CLOWN: Faith, if 'a be not rotten before 'a die—as
we have many pocky corpses nowadays that will   165
scarce hold the laying in—'a will last you some eight
year or nine year. A tanner will last you nine year.
HAMLET: Why he more than another?
FIRST CLOWN: Why, sir, his hide is so tanned with his
trade that 'a will keep out water a great while, and   170
your water is a sore decayer of your whoreson dead
body. [*He picks up a skull.*] Here's a skull now hath
lien you i' th' earth three-and-twenty years.
HAMLET: Whose was it?
FIRST CLOWN: A whoreson mad fellow's it was. Whose   175
do you think it was?
HAMLET: Nay, I know not.
FIRST CLOWN: A pestilence on him for a mad rogue! A
poured a flagon of Rhenish on my head once. This
same skull, sir, was, sir, Yorick's skull, the King's jester.   180
HAMLET: This?
FIRST CLOWN: E'en that.
HAMLET: Let me see. [*He takes the skull.*] Alas, poor Yorick! I knew him, Horatio, a fellow of infinite jest, of
most excellent fancy. He hath bore me on his back a   185

169

thousand times, and now how abhorred in my imagination it is! My gorge rises at it. Here hung those lips
that I have kissed I know not how oft. Where be your
gibes now? Your gambols, your songs, your flashes of
merriment that were wont to set the table on a roar?   190
Not one now, to mock your own grinning? Quite
chopfallen? Now get you to my lady's chamber and
tell her, let her paint an inch thick, to this favor she
must come. Make her laugh at that. Prithee, Horatio,
tell me one thing.   195
HORATIO: What's that, my lord?
HAMLET: Dost thou think Alexander looked o' this fash-
    ion i' th' earth?
HORATIO: E'en so.
HAMLET: And smelt so? Pah!   200

                          [*He puts down the skull.*]

HORATIO: E'en so, my lord.
HAMLET: To what base uses we may return, Horatio!
    Why may not imagination trace the noble dust of Al-
    exander till 'a find it stopping a bunghole?
HORATIO: 'Twere to consider too curiously to consider   205
    so.
HAMLET: No, faith, not a jot; but to follow him thither
    with modesty enough, and likelihood to lead it. As
    thus: Alexander died, Alexander was buried, Alexan-
    der returneth to dust, the dust is earth, of earth we   210
    make loam, and why of that loam whereto he was
    converted might they not stop a beer barrel?
    Imperious Caesar, dead and turned to clay,
    Might stop a hole to keep the wind away.
    O, that the earth which kept the world in awe   215
    Should patch a wall t' expel the winter's flaw!

*Enter King, Queen, Laertes, and the corpse [of Ophelia, in procession, with
Priest, lords, etc.]*

    But soft, but soft awhile! Here comes the King,
    The Queen, the courtiers. Who is this they follow?
    And with such maimèd rites? This doth betoken
    The corpse they follow did with desperate hand   220
    Fordo its own life. 'Twas of some estate.
    Couch we awhile and mark.

    [*He and Horatio conceal themselves. Ophelia's body is taken to the grave.*]

LAERTES: What ceremony else?   225

170

HAMLET: [*To Horatio*]
That is Laertes, a very noble youth. Mark.
LAERTES: What ceremony else?
PRIEST: Her obsequies have been as far enlarged
As we have warranty. Her death was doubtful,
And but that great command o'ersways the order
She should in ground unsanctified been lodged
Till the last trumpet. For charitable prayers,   230
Shards, flints, and pebbles should be thrown on her.
Yet here she is allowed her virgin crants,
Her maiden strewments, and the bringing home
Of bell and burial.
LAERTES: Must there no more be done?   235
PRIEST: No more be done.
We should profane the service of the dead
To sing a requiem and such rest to her
As to peace-parted souls.
LAERTES: Lay her i' th' earth,
And from her fair and unpolluted flesh
May violets spring! I tell thee, churlish priest,   240
A ministering angel shall my sister be
When thou liest howling.
HAMLET: [*To Horatio*] What, the fair Ophelia!
QUEEN: [*Scattering flowers*] Sweets to the sweet! Farewell.
I hoped thou shouldst have been my Hamlet's wife.
I thought thy bride-bed to have decked, sweet maid,   245
And not have strewed thy grave.
LAERTES: O, treble woe
Fall ten times treble on that cursèd head
Whose wicked deed thy most ingenious sense
Deprived thee of!—Hold off the earth awhile,
Till I have caught her once more in mine arms.   250

[*He leaps into the grave and embraces Ophelia.*]

Now pile your dust upon the quick and dead,
Till of this flat mountain you have made
T' o'ertop old Pelion or the skyish head
Of blue Olympus.
HAMLET: [*Coming forward*] What is he whose grief
Bears such an emphasis, whose phrase of sorrow   255
Conjures the wandering stars and makes them stand
Like wonder-wounded hearers? This is I,
Hamlet the Dane.
LAERTES: [*Grappling with him*] The devil take thy soul!
HAMLET: Thou pray'st not well.   260
I prithee, take thy fingers from my throat,
For though I am not splenitive and rash,

171

Yet have I in me something dangerous,
Which let thy wisdom fear. Hold off thy hand.
KING: Pluck them asunder.   265
QUEEN: Hamlet, Hamlet!
ALL: Gentlemen!
HORATIO: Good my lord, be quiet.

                                        [Hamlet and Laertes are parted.]

HAMLET: Why, I will fight with him upon his theme
        Until my eyelids will no longer wag.   270
QUEEN: O my son, what theme?
HAMLET: I loved Ophelia. Forty thousand brothers
        Could not with all their quantity of love
        Make up my sum. What wilt thou do for her?
KING: O, he is mad, Laertes.   275
QUEEN: For love of God, forbear him.
HAMLET: 'Swounds, show me what thou'lt do.
        Woo't weep? Woo't fight. Woo't fast? Woo't tear
            thyself?
        Woo't drink up eisel? Eat a crocodile?
        I'll do 't. Dost come here to whine?   280
        To outface me with leaping in her grave?
        Be buried quick with her, and so will I.
        And if thou prate of mountains, let them throw
        Millions of acres on us, till our ground,
        Singeing his pate against the burning zone,   285
        Make Ossa like a wart! Nay, an thou'lt mouth,
        I'll rant as well as thou.
QUEEN: This is mere madness,
        And thus awhile the fit will work on him;
        Anon, as patient as the female dove
        When that her golden couplets are disclosed,   290
        His silence will sit drooping.
HAMLET: Hear you, sir.
        What is the reason that you use me thus?
        I loved you ever. But it is no matter.
        Let Hercules himself do what he may,
        The cat will mew, and dog will have his day.   295
KING: I pray thee, good Horatio, wait upon him.

                                        Exit Hamlet and Horatio.

[To Laertes.] Strengthen your patience in our last night's
            speech;
We'll put the matter to the present push.—

Good Gertrude, set some watch over your son.—
This grave shall have a living monument.   300
An hour of quiet shortly shall we see;
Till then, in patience our proceeding be.

Exeunt.

ACT V. SCENE II

Enter Hamlet and Horatio.

HAMLET: So much for this, sir; now shall you see the other.
    You do remember all the circumstance?
HORATIO: Remember it, my lord!
HAMLET: Sir, in my heart there was a kind of fighting
    That would not let me sleep. Methought I lay   5
    Worse than the mutines in the bilboes. Rashly,
    And praised be rashness for it—let us know
    Our indiscretion sometimes serves us well
    When our deep plots do pall, and that should learn us
    There's a divinity that shapes our ends,   10
    Rough-hew them how we will—
HORATIO: That is most certain.
HAMLET: Up from my cabin,
    My sea-gown scarfed about me, in the dark
    Groped I to find out them, had my desire,
    Fingered their packet, and in fine withdrew   15
    To mine own room again, making so bold,
    My fears forgetting manners, to unseal
    Their grand commission; where I found, Horatio—
    Ah, royal knavery!—an exact command,
    Larded with many several sorts of reasons   20
    Importing Denmark's health and England's too,
    With, ho! such bugs and goblins in my life,
    That on the supervise, no leisure bated,
    No, not to stay the grinding of the ax,
    My head should be struck off.
HORATIO: Is 't possible?   25
HAMLET: [*Giving a document*]
    Here's the commission. Read it at more leisure.
    But wilt thou hear now how I did proceed?
HORATIO: I beseech you.
HAMLET: Being thus benetted round with villainies—
    Ere I could make a prologue to my brains,   30
    They had begun the play—I sat me down,
    Devised a new commission, wrote it fair.
    I once did hold it, as our statists do,

A baseness to write fair, and labored much
How to forget that learning, but, sir, now   35
It did me yeoman's service. Wilt thou know
Th' effect of what I wrote?
HORATIO: Ay, good my lord.
HAMLET: An earnest conjuration from the King,
As England was his faithful tributary,
As love between them like the palm might flourish,   40
As peace should still her wheaten garland wear
And stand a comma 'tween their amities,
And many suchlike "as"es of great charge,
That on the view and knowing of these contents,
Without debatement further more or less,   45
He should those bearers put to sudden death,
Not shriving time allowed.
HORATIO: How was this sealed?
HAMLET: Why, even in that was heaven ordinant.
I had my father's signet in my purse,
Which was the model of that Danish seal;   50
Folded the writ up in the form of th' other,
Subscribed it, gave 't th' impression, placed it safely,
The changeling never known. Now, the next day
Was our sea flight, and what to this was sequent
Thou knowest already.   55
HORATIO: So Guildenstern and Rosencrantz go to 't.
HAMLET: Why, man, they did make love to this employment.
They are not near my conscience. Their defeat
Does by their own insinuation grow.
'Tis dangerous when the baser nature comes   60
Between the pass and fell incensèd points
Of mighty opposites.
HORATIO: Why, what a king is this!
HAMLET: Does it not, think thee, stand me now upon—
He that hath killed my king and whored my mother,
Popped in between th' election and my hopes,   65
Thrown out his angle for my proper life,
And with such cozenage—is 't not perfect conscience
To quit him with this arm? And is 't not to be damned
To let this canker of our nature come
In further evil?   70
HORATIO: It must be shortly known to him from England
What is the issue of the business there.
HAMLET: It will be short. The interim is mine,
And a man's life's no more than to say "one."
But I am very sorry, good Horatio,   75
That to Laertes I forgot myself,
For by the image of my cause I see
The portraiture of his. I'll court his favors.

174

But, sure, the bravery of his grief did put me
Into a tow'ring passion.
HORATIO: Peace, who comes here?   80

Enter a Courtier [Osric].

OSRIC: Your lordship is right welcome back to Denmark.
HAMLET: I humbly thank you, sir. [*To Horatio.*] Dost
   know this water fly?
HORATIO: No, my good lord.
HAMLET: Thy state is the more gracious, for 'tis a vice to   85
   know him. He hath much land, and fertile. Let a beast
   be lord of beasts, and his crib shall stand at the King's
   mess. 'Tis a chuff, but, as I say, spacious in the pos-
   session of dirt.
OSRIC: Sweet lord, if your lordship were at leisure, I   90
   should impart a thing to you from His Majesty.
HAMLET: I will receive it, sir, with all diligence of spirit.
   Put your bonnet to his right use; 'tis for the head.
OSRIC: I thank your lordship, it is very hot.
HAMLET: No, believe me, 'tis very cold. The wind is   95
   northerly.
OSRIC: It is indifferent cold, my lord, indeed.
HAMLET: But yet methinks it is very sultry and hot for
   my complexion.
OSRIC: Exceedingly, my lord. It is very sultry, as   100
   'twere—I cannot tell how. My lord, His Majesty bade
   me signify to you that 'a has laid a great wager on your
   head. Sir, this is the matter—
HAMLET: I beseech you, remember.

                    [*Hamlet moves him to put on his hat.*]

OSRIC: Nay, good my lord; for my ease, in good faith.   105
   Sir, here is newly come to court Laertes—believe me,
   an absolute gentleman, full of most excellent differ-
   ences, of very soft society and great showing. Indeed,
   to speak feelingly of him, he is the card or calendar of
   gentry, for you shall find in him the continent of what   110
   part a gentleman would see.
HAMLET: Sir, his definement suffers no perdition in
   you, though I know to divide him inventorially
   would dozy th' arithmetic of memory, and yet but yaw
   neither in respect of his quick sail. But, in the verity of 115
   extolment, I take him to be a soul of great article and
   his infusion of such dearth and rareness as, to make
   true diction of him, his semblable is his mirror and
   who else would trace him his umbrage, nothing
   more.   120

175

OSRIC: Your lordship speaks most infallibly of him.

HAMLET: The concernancy, sir? Why do we wrap the
gentleman in our more rawer breath?

OSRIC: Sir?

HORATIO: Is 't not possible to understand in another   125
tongue? You will do 't, sir, really.

HAMLET: What imports the nomination of this gentleman?

OSRIC: Of Laertes?

HORATIO: [*To Hamlet*] His purse is empty already; all 's   130
golden words are spent.

HAMLET: Of him, sir.

OSRIC: I know you are not ignorant—

HAMLET: I would you did, sir. Yet in faith if you did,
it would not much approve me. Well, sir?   135

OSRIC: You are not ignorant of what excellence Laertes
is—

HAMLET: I dare not confess that, lest I should compare
with him in excellence. But to know a man well were
to know himself.   140

OSRIC: I mean, sir, for his weapon; but in the imputa-
tion laid on him by them in his meed, he's unfellowed.

HAMLET: What's his weapon?

OSRIC: Rapier and dagger.

HAMLET: That's two of his weapons—but well.   145

OSRIC: The King, sir, hath wagered with him six Barbary
horses, against the which he has impawned, as I take
it, six French rapiers and poniards, with their assigns,
as girdle, hangers, and so. Three of the carriages, in
faith, are very dear to fancy, very responsive to the   150
hilts, most delicate carriages, and of very liberal conceit.

HAMLET: What call you the carriages?

HORATIO: [*To Hamlet*] I knew you must be edified by
the margent ere you had done.   155

OSRIC: The carriages, sir, are the hangers.

HAMLET: The phrase would be more germane to the
matter if we could carry a cannon by our sides; I would
it might be hangers till then. But, on: six Barbary horses
against six French swords, their assigns, and three lib-   160
eral-conceited carriages; that's the French bet against
the Danish. Why is this impawned, as you call it?

OSRIC: The King, sir, hath laid, sir, that in a dozen
passes between yourself and him, he shall not exceed
you three hits. He hath laid on twelve for nine, and it   165
would come to immediate trial, if your lordship would
vouchsafe the answer.

HAMLET: How if I answer no?

OSRIC: I mean, my lord, the opposition of your person
    in trial. 170
HAMLET: Sir, I will walk here in the hall. If it please His
    Majesty, it is the breathing time of day with me. Let
    the foils be brought, the gentleman willing, and the
    King hold his purpose, I will win for him an I can; if
    not, I will gain nothing but my shame and the odd 175
    hits.
OSRIC: Shall I deliver you so?
HAMLET: To this effect, sir—after what flourish your na-
    ture will.
OSRIC: I commend my duty to your lordship. 180
HAMLET: Yours, yours. [Exit Osric.] 'A does well to
    commend it himself; there are no tongues else for 's
    turn.
HORATIO: This lapwing runs away with the shell on his
    head. 185
HAMLET: 'A did comply with his dug before 'a sucked
    it. Thus has he—and many more of the same breed
    that I know the drossy age dotes on—only got the
    tune of the time and, out of an habit of encounter, a
    kind of yeasty collection, which carries them through 190
    and through the most fanned and winnowed opinions;
    and do but blow them to their trial, the bubbles are
    out.

Enter a Lord.

LORD: My lord, His Majesty commended him to you by
    young Osric, who brings back to him that you attend 195
    him in the hall. He sends to know if your pleasure
    hold to play with Laertes, or that you will take longer
    time.
HAMLET: I am constant to my purposes; they follow the
    King's pleasure. If his fitness speaks, mine is ready; 200
    now or whensoever, provided I be so able as now.
LORD: The King and Queen and all are coming down.
HAMLET: In happy time.
LORD: The Queen desires you to use some gentle enter-
    tainment to Laertes before you fall to play. 205
HAMLET: She well instructs me.

Exit Lord.

HORATIO: You will lose, my lord.
HAMLET: I do not think so. Since he went into France, I
    have been in continual practice; I shall win at the
    odds. But thou wouldst not think how ill all's here 210
    about my heart; but it is no matter.

HORATIO: Nay, good my lord—
HAMLET: It is but foolery, but it is such a kind of gain-
  giving as would perhaps trouble a woman.
HORATIO: If your mind dislike anything, obey it. I will   215
  forestall their repair hither and say you are not fit.
HAMLET: Not a whit, we defy augury. There is special
  providence in the fall of a sparrow. If it be now, 'tis
  not to come; if it be not to come, it will be now; if it
  be not now, yet it will come. The readiness is all. Since   220
  no man of aught he leaves knows, what is 't to leave
  betimes? Let be.

A table prepared. [Enter] trumpets, drums, and officers with cushions; King,
Queen, [Osric,] and all the state; foils, daggers, [and wine borne in;] and Laertes.

KING: Come, Hamlet, come and take this hand from me.

                    [The King puts Laertes's hand into Hamlet's.]

HAMLET: Give me your pardon, sir. I have done you wrong,
  But pardon 't as you are a gentleman.   225
  This presence knows,
  And you must needs have heard, how I am punished
  With a sore distraction. What I have done
  That might your nature, honor, and exception
  Roughly awake, I here proclaim was madness.   230
  Was 't Hamlet wronged Laertes? Never Hamlet.
  If Hamlet from himself be ta'en away.
  And when he's not himself does wrong Laertes,
  Then Hamlet does it not, Hamlet denies it.
  Who does it, then? His madness. If 't be so,   235
  Hamlet is of the faction that is wronged;
  His madness is poor Hamlet's enemy.
  Sir, in this audience,
  Let my disclaiming from a purposed evil
  Free me so far in your most generous thoughts   240
  That I have shot my arrow o'er the house
  And hurt my brother.
LAERTES: I am satisfied in nature,
  Whose motive in this case should stir me most
  To my revenge. But in my terms of honor
  I stand aloof, and will no reconcilement   245
  Till by some elder masters of known honor
  I have a voice and precedent of peace
  To keep my name ungored. But till that time,
  I do receive your offered love like love,
  And will not wrong it.

178

HAMLET: I embrace it freely.   250
    And will this brothers' wager frankly play.—
    Give us the foils. Come on.
LAERTES: Come, one for me.
HAMLET: I'll be your foil, Laertes. In mine ignorance
    Your skill shall, like a star i' the darkest night,
    Stick fiery off indeed.
LAERTES: You mock me, sir.   255
HAMLET: No, by this hand.
KING: Give them the foils, young Osric. Cousin Hamlet,
    You know the wager?
HAMLET: Very well, my lord.
    Your Grace has laid the odds o' the weaker side.
KING: I do not fear it; I have seen you both.   260
    But since he is bettered, we have therefore odds.
LAERTES: This is too heavy. Let me see another.

> [*He exchanges his foil for another.*]

HAMLET: This likes me well. These foils have all a length?

> [*They prepare to play.*]

OSRIC: Ay, my good lord.
KING: Set me the stoups of wine upon that table.   265
    If Hamlet give the first or second hit,
    Or quit in answer of the third exchange,
    Let all the battlements their ordnance fire.
    The King shall drink to Hamlet's better breath,
    And in the cup an union shall he throw   270
    Richer than that which four successive kings
    In Denmark's crown have worn. Give me the cups,
    And let the kettle to the trumpet speak,
    The trumpet to the cannoneer without,
    The cannons to the heavens, the heaven to earth,   275
    "Now the King drinks to Hamlet." Come, begin.

> *Trumpets the while.*

    And you, the judges, bear a wary eye.
HAMLET: Come on, sir.
LAERTES: Come, my lord.

> [*They play. Hamlet scores a hit.*]

HAMLET: One.   280
LAERTES: No.
HAMLET: Judgment.

OSRIC: A hit, a very palpable hit.

Drum, trumpets, and shot. Flourish. A piece goes off.

LAERTES: Well, again.
KING: Stay, give me drink. Hamlet, this pearl is thine.

[He throws a pearl in Hamlet's cup, and drinks.]

Here's to thy health. Give him the cup.   285
HAMLET: I'll play this bout first. Set it by awhile.
    Come. [*They play.*] Another hit; what say you?
LAERTES: A touch, a touch, I do confess 't.
KING: Our son shall win.
QUEEN: He's fat and scant of breath.
    Here, Hamlet, take my napkin, rub thy brows.   290
    The Queen carouses to thy fortune, Hamlet.
HAMLET: Good madam!
KING: Gertrude, do not drink.
QUEEN: I will, my lord, I pray you pardon me.

[She drinks.]

KING: [*Aside*] It is the poisoned cup. It is too late.   295
HAMLET: I dare not drink yet, madam; by and by.
QUEEN: Come, let me wipe thy face.
LAERTES: [*To the King*] My lord, I'll hit him now.
KING: I do not think 't.
LAERTES: [*Aside*] And yet it is almost against my conscience.
HAMLET: Come, for the third, Laertes. You do but dally.   300
    I pray you, pass with your best violence;
    I am afeard you make a wanton of me.
LAERTES: Say you so? Come on.

[They play.]

OSRIC: Nothing neither way.
LAERTES: Have at you now!

*[Laertes wounds Hamlet; then, in scuffling, they change rapiers,
and Hamlet wounds Laertes.]*

KING: Part them! They are incensed.   305
HAMLET: Nay, come, again.

[The Queen falls.]

OSRIC: Look to the Queen there, ho!

180

HORATIO: They bleed on both sides. How is it, my lord?
OSRIC: How is 't, Laertes?
LAERTES: Why, as a woodcock to mine own springe, Osric;
I am justly killed with mine own treachery.   310
HAMLET: How does the Queen?
KING: She swoons to see them bleed.
QUEEN: No, no, the drink, the drink—O my dear Hamlet—
The drink, the drink! I am poisoned.

                                                        [*She dies.*]

HAMLET: O villainy! Ho, let the door be locked!
Treachery! Seek it out.   315

                                        [*Laertes falls.*] *Exit Osric.*

LAERTES: It is here, Hamlet. Hamlet, thou art slain.
No med'cine in the world can do thee good;
In thee there is not half an hour's life.
The treacherous instrument is in thy hand,
Unbated and envenomed. The foul practice   320
Hath turned itself on me. Lo, here I lie,
Never to rise again. Thy mother's poisoned.
I can no more. The King, the King's to blame.
HAMLET: The point envenomed too? Then, venom, to thy work.

                                                [*He stabs the King.*]

ALL: Treason! Treason!   325
KING: O, yet defend me, friends! I am but hurt.
HAMLET: [*Forcing the King to drink*]
Here, thou incestuous, murderous, damnèd Dane,
Drink off this potion. Is thy union here?
Follow my mother.

                                                [*The King dies.*]

LAERTES: He is justly served.
It is a poison tempered by himself.   330
Exchange forgiveness with me, noble Hamlet.
Mine and my father's death come not upon thee,
Nor thine on me!

                                                        [*He dies.*]

HAMLET: Heaven make thee free of it! I follow thee.
I am dead, Horatio. Wretched Queen, adieu!   335
You that look pale and tremble at this chance,

That are but mutes or audience to this act,
Had I but time—as this fell sergeant, Death,
Is strict in his arrest—O, I could tell you—
But let it be. Horatio, I am dead;   340
Thou livest. Report me and my cause aright
To the unsatisfied.
HORATIO: Never believe it.
I am more an antique Roman than a Dane.
Here's yet some liquor left.

> [*He attempts to drink from the poisoned cup. Hamlet prevents him.*]

HAMLET: As thou'rt a man,
Give me the cup! Let go! By heaven, I'll ha' 't.   345
O God, Horatio, what a wounded name,
Things standing thus unknown, shall I leave behind me!
If thou didst ever hold me in thy heart,
Absent thee from felicity awhile,
And in this harsh world draw thy breath in pain   350
To tell my story. (*A march afar off [and a volley within].*)
What warlike noise is this?

Enter Osric.

OSRIC: Young Fortinbras, with conquest come from Poland,
To th' ambassadors of England gives
This warlike volley.
HAMLET: O, I die, Horatio!
The potent poison quite o'ercrows my spirit.   355
I cannot live to hear the news from England ,
But I do prophesy th' election lights
On Fortinbras. He has my dying voice.
So tell him, with th' occurrents more and less
Which have solicited—the rest is silence.   360

> [*He dies.*]

HORATIO: Now cracks a noble heart. Good night, sweet prince,
And flights of angles sing thee to thy rest!

> [*March within.*]

Why does the drum come hither?

Enter Fortinbras, with the [English] Ambassadors [with drums, colors, and attendants].

FORTINBRAS: Where is this sight?

182

HORATIO: What is it you would see?
If aught of woe or wonder, cease your search.   365
FORTINBRAS: This quarry cries on havoc. O proud Death,
What feast is toward in thine eternal cell,
That thou so many princes at a shot
So bloodily hast struck?
FIRST AMBASSADOR: The sight is dismal,
And our affairs from England come too late.   370
The ears are senseless that should give us hearing,
To tell him his commandment is fulfilled,
That Rosencrantz and Guildenstern are dead.
Where should we have our thanks?   ·
HORATIO: Not from his mouth,
Had it th' ability of life to thank you.   375
He never gave commandment for their death.
But since, so jump upon this bloody question,
You from the Polack wars, and you from England,
Are here arrived, give order that these bodies
High on a stage be placèd to the view,   380
And let me speak to th' yet unknowing world
How these things came about. So shall you hear
Of carnal, bloody, and unnatural acts,
Of accidental judgments, casual slaughters,
Of deaths put on by cunning and forced cause,   385
And, in this upshot, purposes mistook
Fall'n on th' inventors' heads. All this can I
Truly deliver.
FORTINBRAS: Let us haste to hear it,
And call the noblest to the audience.
For me, with sorrow I embrace my fortune.   390
I have some rights of memory in this kingdom,
Which now to claim my vantage doth invite me.
HORATIO: Of that I shall have also cause to speak,
And from his mouth whose voice will draw on more.
But let this same be presently performed,   395
Even while men's minds are wild, lest more mischance
On plots and errors happen.
FORTINBRAS: Let four captains
Bear Hamlet, like a soldier, to the stage,
For he was likely, had he been put on,
To have proved most royal; and for his passage,   400
The soldiers' music and the rite of war
Speak loudly for him.
Take up the bodies. Such a sight as this
Becomes the field, but here shows much amiss.
Go bid the soldiers shoot.   405

Exeunt [marching, bearing off the dead bodies; a peal of ordnance is shot off].

183